Innocence Betrayed

This book is dedicated to all children
– especially Fleur, Hugo, Alex and Daniel.

Innocence Betrayed

Paedophilia, the Media
and Society

Jon Silverman and
David Wilson

polity

Copyright © Jon Silverman and David Wilson 2002

The right of Jon Silverman and David Wilson to be identified as authors of this work has been asserted in accordance with the Copyright, Designs and Patents Act 1988.

First published in 2002 by Polity Press in association with Blackwell Publishing Ltd

Editorial office:
Polity Press
65 Bridge Street
Cambridge CB2 1UR, UK

Marketing and production:
Blackwell Publishing Ltd
108 Cowley Road
Oxford OX4 1JF, UK

Distributed in the USA by
Blackwell Publishing Inc.
350 Main Street
Malden, MA 02148, USA

A catalogue record for this book is available from the British Library.

Library of Congress Cataloging-in-Publication Data
Silverman, Jon.
    Innocence betrayed : paedophilia, the media, and society / Jon Silverman and David Wilson.
        p. cm.
    Includes bibliographical references and index.
    ISBN 0-7456-2888-5 – ISBN 0-7456-2889-3 (pbk.)
    1. Child sexual abuse–Great Britain.   2. Pedophilia–Great Britain.   3. Child molesters–Great Britain.   4. Criminal registers–Great Britain.   5. Mass media and crime–Great Britain.   I. Wilson, David, 1957–   II. Title.
    HV6570.4.G7 S54 2002
    364.15'3—dc21

                                                                    2002006379

Typeset in 10.5 on 12.5pt Berling
by Graphicraft Limited, Hong Kong
Printed in Great Britain by MPG Books, Bodmin, Cornwall

Contents

Acknowledgements

We would like to thank all the people who very kindly gave up their time while we were conducting the research for this book, particularly the staff of HMPs Grendon and Wayland; colleagues at UCE, especially John Rouse, who made a small travel grant available; Jim Reynolds and Terry Jones; Gill Mackenzie; the Toronto Sexual Abuse Squad, especially Wendy Leaver; the Circles Project in Toronto, especially Eileen Henderson; Barbara McCalla; the Barrow–Cadbury Trust; and all the people who prefer to remain anonymous but without whom this book could not have been completed. Finally, we would like to thank Anne and Jackie.

Introduction

The paedophile is the bogeyman of our age. The very word itself has become a conduit for fear and public loathing, often beyond all moderation. Indeed, despite the fact that the overwhelming majority of paedophiles are male, commentators reach easily for parallels with a reviled figure from a bygone age – the witch. While we haven't yet reinvented the ducking stool or trial by water, we have found a pretty effective 21st-century equivalent in trial by newspaper. And, after being named and shamed, the "guilty" are hounded from the community by a mob baying for blood.

We know, of course, that crime, or the fear of crime, has periodically triggered a response which the criminologist Stan Cohen famously described as a "moral panic" (Cohen, 1972). Whether it is the footpads of the mid-nineteenth century, the muggers of the 1970s or today's young mobile-phone thieves, society occasionally whips itself into a fervour entirely disproportionate to the threat. But paedophilia has generated a reaction of an entirely different kind. It is not just the street marches and sloganeering, or the breaking of windows and firebombing. These are of course bad enough, but more insidious still is the way that the public debate appears to have been hijacked by the forces of prejudice and misinformation, to the extent that what is important for the protection of our children is downplayed, and what is marginal is elevated beyond all sense. This is what angers us, and one of our motives for writing this book was better to inform the public debate about how best to protect our children from the threat of predatory paedophiles. Thus we spend more time looking at practical policies than we do in an arid intellectual rebuttal of arguments with which we disagree.

In researching this book, we have interviewed paedophiles, both in prison and in the community. We have interviewed therapists, police, prison and probation officers, Home Office policy-makers, victims of sexual abuse and those who have protested in the streets. We have been to Canada to look at how "ordinary" people with an extraordinary commitment to their fellow human beings have made a difference to recidivism rates among convicted paedophiles. And we have examined in detail the impact of the Internet on the distribution of paedophile imagery and its connection to the sexual exploitation and abuse of children. Using confidential Home Office material, we tell the inside story of how the *News of the World*'s naming and shaming campaign caused panic in Whitehall. And unrivalled access to the prison service's Sex Offender Treatment Programme sheds new light on the techniques used to prepare paedophiles for release.

Access to these various individuals or groups was facilitated by a network of professional contacts in the media and academia. Some of these contacts did not want to be named, and we have respected their wishes. Access to HMPs Grendon and Wayland was expedited through personal negotiation with the governors, staff and prisoners of these two institutions, and was again facilitated by a personal network, given that one of the authors had previously worked as a prison governor. Gaining access to released paedophiles was clearly more problematic, and required patience and persistence. Typically a therapist would recommend a contact, and that contact – over a period of some time – would put us in touch with others who were prepared to be interviewed. Throughout this process we attempted to triangulate any information that we received from these contacts by checking specific details with therapists or with criminal justice professionals.

The starting-point for our analysis was the sequence of very public events that followed the murder of eight-year-old Sarah Payne in July 2000. First came the identification of convicted paedophiles by the *News of the World*; then the vigilante-inspired violence in Portsmouth and elsewhere; the reaction (or, as we point out, non-reaction) of politicians and policy-makers; and finally the subsequent debate about legislative changes along the lines of "Megan's Law" in the USA to inform parents of a paedophile in their community. The lesson we draw is that society will never achieve protection by "naming and shaming", which in many cases makes paedophiles "invisible" – the exact opposite of the aim behind community notification. Nor will there be measurable progress until the public debate is no longer shaped by exaggerated fears of "stranger danger" at the expense of the epidemic of inter-familial sexual abuse, which rarely gets disclosed, let alone adequately represented in the criminal justice statistics.

Many of our arguments about the hysteria surrounding paedophiles would apply equally to other forms of violent crime (and, make no mistake, child sex abuse is a violent crime). After all, screaming headlines which precipitate ill-thought-out ministerial announcements, and sometimes knee-jerk decision-making, are not a new phenomenon. But there is a vital difference with child sex abuse. If you take rape and indecent assault, for example, it is clear that an intensive public education campaign over the last decade has transformed attitudes and led to a big rise in the reporting of offences. But the paedophile behaviour that comes to the attention of the criminal justice system, or even of other social agencies, is but the tip of the iceberg. And we believe that the only form of disclosure which it is important to press for is the disclosure of unacceptable behaviour by victims, and those close to them – not the disclosure to the public of information about convicted offenders, which is calculated to inflame prejudice and provoke violence.

Self-evidently, this book is a collaboration, but it is a highly unusual one. Our writing reflects three different disciplines – criminology, penal practice and the media – all with a strong bearing on the paedophile debate. The techniques we employ range from the narrative drive of New Journalism to the academic rigour of criminology. Our styles are different, but we hope that it is a union of strengths, and uniquely suited to the subject matter. Nor do we underestimate the gendered nature of what it is we are investigating – after all, as we have said, the majority of paedophiles are men. As a consequence, we have attempted to balance any gender blindness or bias on our part by interviewing, wherever possible, female therapists, psychologists, police and prison officers, and victims of abuse. Finally, on a more personal level, we are both fathers, and we never lose sight of the pain that is at the core of child sex abuse.

The most obvious research technique that we employ throughout the book is interview. However, as we have implied above, the use that we make of these interviews reflects our respective backgrounds and training. Thus, for example, interviews are used to prompt the narrative drive by linking one section to another, and are employed to illustrate ideas, feelings or situations. On the other hand, we also use interviews to ground our theory in the lived experiences of those who have been abused, or who have abused, or with those who work with paedophiles. Thus in this respect our interest has been to see beyond newspaper headlines, and find similarities or patterns in what those who are particularly experienced in these matters – although often from very different backgrounds – think about "community notification", "naming and shaming", and how best to protect our children.

As such we oppose the campaign for "community notification", whose flag-bearer is the *News of the World*, and as a result we will no doubt face criticism. Indeed, we have already glimpsed some of the difficulties of standing against the tide of a national prejudice. In conducting our research, we tracked a paedophile from his release from prison and interviewed him over several months as he tried to find his place in the community. Much of his story appears in chapter 6. At one point, Phil (not his real name) described how he had changed his hair colour because he was anxious that all his efforts to integrate were about to be undermined by being "named and shamed" in the *News of the World*. One of the authors mentioned this in a regular column he writes for a regional newspaper – the *Birmingham Post*. Perhaps predictably, this column attracted the critical attention of the *News of the World*, which urged readers with strong views on the subject to fax the university that employs the author. It helpfully published a fax number for the Faculty of Law and Social Sciences.

The faxes which duly arrived reveal a little of the obsession and bigotry that we have so far described only tentatively, and which propels some people to take to the streets to harass suspected paedophiles, and to daub slogans on walls and doors threatening to castrate and kill. Of course these faxes are not a scientific sample – for example, there is no way of determining age, social class or personal histories, though, if the names of many of the writers are genuine, they are overwhelmingly male. Later in the book, we explore the psychology of some of those who have clambered aboard the anti-paedophile bandwagon (as well as their politics, since there is evidence that far-right groups such as the National Front and British National Party have sought to exploit the issue for ulterior motives). But, to give a flavour of this potent brew, here are a few of the sentiments expressed:

I live every day feeling sick and saddened about Sarah Payne and other children hurt by sick paedophiles. Why should they be protected? They don't deserve the air they breathe. To me, anyone who does not support Sarah Payne's Law must be in some way the same as paedophiles.

Let's hope when they come for your kids you will be as understanding! We should lock you up also as mentally disturbed.

You asshole. Why is it I get the feeling you're a fucking paedophile at heart. Have you got ideas of touching little children? Don't ever get the idea of coming to Liverpool to give one of your sick speeches, as it will be your last. Assholes like you should be executed on the spot.

It is important to emphasize what this book is not about. We do not, for example, describe any of the current debates about the changing nature of childhood, although we draw attention to this theme in Chapter 3. Similarly, those with a specialist interest in cognitive behavioural therapy, cognitive skills, or the risk assessment of sex offenders will find this book of only passing interest, for we use aspects of these issues simply where they throw light onto the main focus of the book, or as a way of providing necessary background detail. Nor have we chosen to deal in detail with cases of sexual abuse of children in formal residential settings, such as special schools or religious institutions. This issue deserves – and in some cases (such as the North Wales children's home scandal) has had – its own consideration. Where we have touched on "historical" cases of child abuse which have been under recent investigation by the police, it is to underline one of our key themes – the unplanned way in which even the mere suspicion of paedophile activity has become such a priority for the criminal justice system. Nevertheless, in Chapter 5, we note the growing concern about false allegations of abuse – and, incidentally, both authors attended a conference on the subject in September 2001. Those who have a particular interest in this issue will find suggestions for further reading in the bibliography at the end of the book.

Some ten or fifteen years ago, a book on sex offending and society would have spent some time looking at the trade in explicitly pornographic videos. But in the 1990s the means of communication were transformed beyond recognition by the Internet. Law enforcement agencies such as the National Criminal Intelligence Service, Interpol, Europol and the FBI say the Internet is without doubt the principal conduit for child abuse imagery. But here, too, we delve behind the received wisdom and explore different angles. If the anonymity of the Internet makes it attractive for abusers, could not that same anonymity be turned to advantage to stem the tide? Certainly, in the United States they believe so. In a number of cases, FBI agents posing as children have entered chat rooms and enticed paedophiles into meetings which have led to arrests. In the UK, there are legal rules which prevent the police acting as *agents provocateurs*, but we reveal a far more proactive approach than has been traditional in UK law enforcement.

On an important housekeeping note, we should emphasize that ethical considerations have been at the heart of how we have conducted our research and what we have written. At the most obvious level, this means we have not paid for any interviews or for access to those we have interviewed. However, as is standard, we have also promised anonymity to those who asked for it, and we have deliberately concealed details so that their identities will remain secret. (Indeed we have also chosen not to publish the names or telephone numbers of those who faxed to us.) On the other hand, we made it clear that, if we felt that any information indicated that an interviewee was still offending, we would have ended the interview and reported the matter to the police. As it happens, we never felt the need to end an interview.

We intend this book to have the broadest possible readership, so, while we have infused the text with scholarly insight and rigour, citing sources where necessary, we have written it to be inclusive. No doubt we could have incorporated more academic sources and cited a greater number of references so as to place the book more firmly within a scholarly tradition. However, at least we agree with the tabloids on one thing – that this is too important an issue to be left to the "professionals", whether they be academics, journalists or criminal justice personnel. On 1 April 2001, new arrangements for the assessment and management of sex offenders came into force under the banner of the Criminal Justice and Court Services Act. For the first time, criminal justice agencies were under a statutory duty to consider "community issues and concerns" when making their decisions. It marks a new phase in the troubled debate about paedophiles. This book is offered as a clear-eyed contribution to that debate.

1

A Short History of Sex Offending

The law on sexual offences is confused and confusing. It is comprehensive but incoherent and has many anomalities that need resolving.
Paul Boateng, former Home Office minister

These first two chapters seek to place our current obsession with sex
offenders and paedophiles in a historical perspective, and to provide
a context within which to understand better those other issues and
themes which we will develop later. In this first chapter we spend
some time looking at how Britain has attempted to combat sexual
offending, which is also placed within a historical context. For, in
looking at the past, we attempt to see if our present approach –
symbolically characterized by the Sex Offender Register – has been
tried before. In doing so we provide an analysis of one largely for-
gotten incident from the Victorian period – the garrotting panic
of 1862, which culminated in the Garrotters' Act of 1863 and the
registration of "ticket of leave" men. However, we also provide
a contemporary context for our later chapters. We present, for example, a statistical breakdown of the extent of sexual offending
between 1987 and 1997, as gleaned from Home Office figures,
and in doing so begin to deconstruct what it is that we mean by the
term "sex offending". In this respect we introduce the concept of
"consent". Above all in this first chapter we attempt to see how
those activities that come to be called "crime" are neither fixed nor
unchanging, but vary over time and between cultures. As such our
story starts in April 2001, with a local trader who becomes known
as "the metric martyr".

In April 2001 Steven Thornburn, a 36-year-old greengrocer in Sunderland, was found guilty of having sold, several months previously, a pound of bananas that had been weighed on imperial scales to an official from the city's Trading Standards Office, who had posed as a customer. Thorburn's imperial-only weighing scales were subsequently confiscated, given that his refusal to switch to a set of metric scales breached a European directive which had been incorporated into the Weights and Measures Act 1985. Thus he had broken the law – he had committed a "crime" – for which he was given a six-month conditional discharge and a heavy fine.

Thornburn's prosecution is a very good example to remind us that what we call "crime" changes over time, and can vary between countries. Thus, it had been perfectly permissible for Thornburn to have sold bananas weighed only in pounds prior to the adoption of European legislation into English law, and it is still permissible to sell bananas in pounds in various other countries of the world – including Jamaica, the biggest exporter of the fruit. In this case a "crime" – using an imperial-only weighing machine – has been invented, and as such becomes just the latest of a long list of "new" crimes over the last twenty years; these include not wearing a crash helmet on a motorbike, or a seat belt in a car where they are fitted, selling beef on the bone, stalking a former partner, or "hacking" into someone else's computer. Equally, "crimes" can be abolished. Thus, for example, a range of sexual behaviours which had previously been "criminal" are now perfectly legal – such as consenting homosexual behaviour between men over the age of sixteen – an area we discuss more fully below.

The key element in all of this is power – the power to create "crime". Clearly we do not all possess the power to label behaviours with which we might disagree as "crime", nor do we all have the power to remove that label once it has been applied to behaviours in which we might engage or of which we might approve. This power resides largely in the hands of politicians who create and judges who interpret the law, which is in turn the responsibility of our police, and others (including trading standards officers), to enforce. However, politicians do not exercise this power in isolation. Rather, they often respond directly to various pressures and anxieties within society, which at certain times can become focused on a particular event, group or issue, which ultimately forces those with power "to do something".

Moral panics and deviancy amplification

Two criminologists, Stan Cohen and the late Leslie Wilkins, offer us several helpful ways of understanding those processes at work when society demands that "something should be done" about the activities of certain groups or individuals, eventually leading to the criminalization of the activities of those groups or individuals. Wilkins (1964), for example, employs the description of "deviancy amplification" to describe what happens when society chooses to outlaw a particular group and then isolate that group from the normal functions of society. Thus, he describes how being isolated allows such a group to develop its own norms and values, which society thereafter perceives as even more deviant than before. In turn this encourages even more social reaction against the group, which becomes still further isolated, and in an ever-increasing cycle of deviance and crime the group becomes more and more criminally orientated. The key to what Wilkins describes is to understand that crime increases as a result of social controls on the group being effective, not as a result of controls on the group having failed.

His theory of deviancy amplification is difficult to test empirically, and Wilkins tells us little about why certain deviant activities become amplified as opposed to others, or how amplification would stop. However, Stan Cohen (1972) argues that, at times of wider social unease or rapid change, "folk devils" and "moral panics" serve to create a sense of control over those events, individuals or groups who appear to threaten the status quo. He bases his analyses on research that he conducted into the activities of working-class London youths who gathered together at Clacton in Essex over the Easter Bank Holiday in 1964. As so often happens in England, the weather was bad; the youths got bored and seem to have engaged in minor acts of vandalism. This became front-page news, with claims being made that the youths had rampaged through Clacton, and that there had been running battles between "Mods" and "Rockers" – even though neither "Mods" nor "Rockers" were "new" ("news" is, after all, the plural of "new"). The media attention that was given to this reporting led to more intensified policing, and also served to create a more coherent sense of being a "Mod" or a "Rocker", which in turn served to polarize these two groups even further – leading to a greater number of arrests, and which thus served to justify the original reporting. Thus, in all of this, it is important to recognize the central role that the media plays in publicizing the activities of the group that is causing disquiet – in this case young people with disposable income – and how it shapes debate by providing further information, which serves to reinforce the original reporting. Above all Cohen suggests that this scare became news as it symbolized wider anxieties about young people, and that "Mods" and "Rockers" served as a specific scapegoat for these more general worries.

From our recent criminological history Mike Levi argues that there have been moral panics about mugging, battered women, rape, racial violence, the ritual Satanic abuse of children, rural violence, dangerous dogs, and assaults on the police. However, in using this concept of moral panic further we have chosen to look at an incident from our Victorian past, given that aspects of the reaction to these incidents throw some light onto our contemporary approach to paedophiles – in particular, the use of a sex offender register.

The garrotting panic of 1862

In the winter of 1862 London was gripped by what *The Times* described as "a new variety of crime", and as a result was in the midst of a "reign of terror" (all quotes taken from Pearson, 1983: 128–55). What this new crime amounted to was a form of robbery whereby the victim was temporarily incapacitated by an assailant, who had approached from behind, while an accomplice effected the robbery from the front as the victim was being choked. No one likes to be robbed, but robberies in London were hardly new. However, what made matters worse was the fact that one of the first victims of this "new" crime happened to be Hugh Pilkington MP, who was attacked and robbed as he walked from the House of Commons to the Reform Club. This seemed to act as a "trigger device", and newspaper editorial after newspaper editorial railed against the garrotters; *Punch* in particular provided its readers with advice on how to avoid being garrotted by using a vast array of all sorts of ingenious gadgets. What's more, the newspapers knew who was behind this wave of garrottings – the "ticket of leave" men.

In the middle years of the nineteenth century, and in particular with transportation to Australia ending in 1857, Londoners had to get used to something which they hadn't had to deal with before in any great numbers – prisoners being released from jail back into the community. The Penal Servitude Act of 1853, for example, while it had increased prison sentences, had also created a system of licensing for the release of discharged prisoners known as "ticket of leave" (c.f. Thomas, 2000: 40–4). Not only that, but the mood of the time was optimistic about how prisoners could be reformed through the discipline of the new penitentiaries, and correspondingly there was less emphasis on physical punishments such as whipping, flogging and hanging. As a consequence this period would see public hangings come to an end in 1868, and flogging abolished for prisoners in 1861.

Ultimately the Garrotters' Act was passed in July 1863, but a series of other pieces of legislation, such as the Penal Servitude Act of 1864 and the Habitual Criminals Act of 1869, were more important as they were aimed directly at curbing the activities and freedoms of the ticket of leave men. Thus, for example, under the Penal Servitude Act there was a requirement that ticket of leave men should report to the police within three days of leaving prison, and thereafter on a monthly basis, or within forty-eight hours if they changed their address. Thomas (2000: 42) reports that this system of registration did not work, and that the police did not, for example, have a central register to which they could refer. The Habitual Criminals Act of 1869 repealed the ticket of leave arrangements – except for those with two felony convictions (perhaps an early example of "two strikes and you're out") – and introduced a new national register of offenders, known as the Habitual Criminals Register. The register applied to England, Wales and Ireland, and was extended to Scotland through the Prevention of Crimes Act of 1871. The register was held at New Scotland Yard, and was meant to be regularly updated. Indeed a Convict Supervision Office was created for this purpose, but eventually, in 1910, this form of police surveillance was dismantled by Winston Churchill while he was home secretary. Petrow (1994: 82) sums up the success or otherwise of the Habitual Criminals Register:

> On balance police supervision, while theoretically valuable, has been practically useless. It helped the police manufacture a criminal class, without really deterring criminals or diminishing crime.

As with the moral panic about Mods and Rockers which we described above, the important point to grasp is that legislation aimed at the

11

ticket of leave men merely became a symbol of wider anxieties in society, and in this particular case was concerned with articulating a devout opposition to penal reform and the possibility of rehabilitation. As Geoffrey Pearson (1983: 152) has put it, "the people who created The Garrotters Act, together with the gentlemen who egged them on from the sidelines, helped to fashion the vocabulary of objections to penal reform which remain with us to this day." Thus the issue was not so much that there were ticket of leave men – or Mods and Rockers – but rather that they came to symbolize dramatic change to the established order and received opinion. Change creates unease and anxiety, and in an effort to regain control over that anxiety the demand that "something should be done" becomes all-pervasive. We will return to this theme when we consider the Sex Offender Register below, given that there are echoes there with the response to ticket of leave men.

These opening sections of this first chapter have attempted to introduce a variety of concepts. First we have attempted to show how what we call "crime" is neither fixed nor unchanging, and we have introduced the idea of power being exercised when crime is created or abolished. In this respect we have used two criminological theories – moral panic and deviancy amplification – to show how society's response to certain groups that are seen to be deviant might in fact make matters worse rather than better, and how this response is often based on wider anxieties which become fixed on these groups. We have introduced the concept of power when thinking about how "crime" is either created or abolished. Finally, we have attempted to use a historical example to throw light on all of these themes, but we have so far avoided any concerted discussion about sexual offending. We turn to this issue now.

Sex and sex offending

In the same way that crime in relation to not wearing a seat belt, or hacking into another person's computer, or even selling bananas by the pound, can be created, so too can crime in relation to a range of sexual behaviours be invented, or indeed abolished. Thus, for example, Donald West (1987: 1) has pointed out that any form of sexual expression other than in "the missionary position", between a "man and wife" for the purpose of producing children, was once an

12

offence against canon law, and a sin in the eyes of the Christian Church. According to Catholic teachings, reinforced by a papal statement in 1976, masturbation was a sin, and in the nineteenth century there was a flourishing trade in mechanical restraints to prevent children playing with their genitals. Before the passage of the Sexual Offences Act of 1967, all homosexual contacts between men in England and Wales were criminal acts punishable by imprisonment, and the law did not recognize the concept of rape within marriage. This latter example should also remind us that there are "public" and "private" spheres to sexual offending, and so, for example, the law decriminalizing homosexual activities stipulated that these must be "in private", without defining what that meant. Thus, in 1997 seven men were prosecuted in Bolton for engaging in homosexual activities within a private household, but in the presence of others, which meant that these activities were no longer considered to be private (*The Guardian*, 23 January 1998).

However, no one now seriously questions the legality of sexual behaviour between consenting heterosexual adults in a variety of positions, and not just for procreation. Nor do we seek to stop young people masturbating. Equally, the law recognizes homosexual behaviour between adults – although there is still an ongoing debate about reducing the age of consent from eighteen to sixteen (see below), and since 1988 in Scotland and 1992 in England and Wales the common law has recognized that rape can take place within marriage. However, writing some time ago, Donald West came to the conclusion that "our sex laws are less than satisfactory" (West, 1987: 15), and he has latterly found support for this position in the unlikely guise of Paul Boateng, former minister of state at the Home Office. In introducing the terms of reference for a review of sexual offences, Mr Boateng commented that:

> The law on sexual offences is confused and confusing. It is compre-
> hensive but incoherent and has many anomalies that need resolving.
> Many of the offences were created a long time ago and reflect the
> social and legal system of their time . . . The law must be brought up
> to date, both to take on board human rights issues and to reflect the
> better understanding we now have of patterns of sexual abuse. (Quoted
> in Thomas, 2000: 7)

Taking this one stage further, we begin to see what Mr Boateng was meaning if we look at some of the numerous lists that have been

---

Table 1.1 A sexual offence (England and Wales)

"Sexual offence" means any of the following:

- an offence under the Sexual Offences Act 1956, other than an offence under section 30, 31, or 33 to 36 of that Act;
- an offence under section 128 of the Mental Health Act 1959;
- an offence under the Indecency with Children Act 1960;
- an offence under section 9 of the Theft Act 1968 of burglary with intent to commit rape;
- an offence under section 54 of the Criminal Law Act 1977;
- an offence under the Protection of Children Act 1978;
- an offence under section 1 of the Criminal Law Act 1977 of conspiracy to commit any of the offences mentioned above;
- an offence under section 1 of the Criminal Attempts Act 1981 of attempting to commit any of those offences;
- an offence of inciting another to commit any of those offences.

---

drawn up about sexual offending, and which are used for various purposes. Thus, for sentencing purposes there exists a list in the Criminal Justice Act 1991 for England and Wales (see table 1.1) and another for the Criminal Procedure (Scotland) Act 1995. There is a list in the Sex Offenders Act 1997 for those offenders who will have to register, but it is actually subdivided into three lists – one for England and Wales, one for Scotland and another for Northern Ireland. These lists should not be confused with the more long-standing "Schedule 1" list of the Children and Young Persons Act 1933, which enumerates all the offences it is possible to commit against a child (see table 1.2).

In short, none of these lists has the same content, which gives some flavour to the difficulty of defining a sexual offence. Further insight into these difficulties can be gleaned by looking at the issue of consent, which, as Thomas (2000: 7) reminds us, "is central to defining sexual offending".

At a most basic level "consent" is often simply equated with the "age of consent" – the age at which children and young people are able legally to agree to participate in sexual activity. For hetero-sexuals the age of consent was fixed at ten in 1285, but in the mid-Victorian period this was raised first in 1875 to thirteen and thereafter in 1885, by the Criminal Law Amendment Act, to sixteen. (Of note: this Act also made illegal acts of gross indecency between males – and was famously used to prosecute Oscar Wilde.)

Table 1.2 Offences listed in Schedule 1 to the Children and Young Persons Act 1933

Common Law Offences:
- the murder of a child or young person under 18
- common assault and battery

Offences Against the Persons Act 1861:
- s.5 Manslaughter of a child or young person under 18
- s.27 The abandonment or exposure of a child under two so as to endanger its life or health

Infant Life (Preservation) Act 1929:
- s.1 Child destruction

Children and Young Persons Act 1933:
- s.1 Cruelty to (including assault, ill treatment or neglect) a person under 16
- s.3 Allowing a person under 16 to be in a brothel
- s.4 causing or allowing a person under 16 to be used for begging
- s.11 Exposing a child under seven to risk of burning
- s.23 Allowing a person under 16 to take part in a dangerous performance

Infanticide Act 1938:
- s.1 Infanticide

Sexual Offences Act 1965:
- s.1 Rape (or attempted rape) of a girl aged under 18
- s.2 Procurement (or attempted procurement) of a girl under 18 by threats
- s.3 Procurement of a girl under 18 by false pretences
- s.4 Administering drugs to a girl under 18 to obtain or facilitate intercourse
- s.5 Intercourse (or attempted intercourse) with a girl under 13
- s.6 Intercourse (or attempted intercourse) with a girl between 13 and 16
- s.7 Intercourse (or attempted intercourse) with a mentally deficient girl under 18
- s.10 Incest (or attempt to commit incest) by a man against a female, where the victim is under 18
- s.11 Incest (or attempt to commit incest) by a woman, where the victim is under 18
- s.12 Buggery (or attempt to commit buggery) with a person under 18
- s.13 Indecency between men where one or both is under 18

Table 1.2 *(cont'd)*

- s.14 Indecent assault on a girl under 18
- s.15 Indecent assault on a male under 18
- s.16 Assault with intent to commit buggery
- s.19 Abduction of an unmarried girl under 18 from a parent or guardian
- s.20 Abduction of an unmarried girl under 16 from a parent or guardian
- s.22 Causing (or attempting to cause) prostitution of a girl under 18
- s.23 Procuring (or attempted procuration) of a girl under 18
- s.24 Detention of a girl under 18 in a brothel or other premises
- s.25 Permitting a girl under 13 to use premises for intercourse
- s.26 Permitting a girl between 13 and 16 to use premises for intercourse
- s.28 Causing or encouraging prostitution of, intercourse with, or indecent assault on, a girl under 16

Indecency with Children Act 1960:
- s.1 Indecent conduct towards a child under 14

Suicide Act 1961:
- s.2 Aiding, abetting, counselling or procuring the suicide of a person under 18

Other Offences:
Any offence involving bodily injury to a person under 18

The pressure to increase the age of consent in 1885 was prompted by a series of popular campaigning articles in the *Pall Mall Gazette*, edited by William T. Stead, which drew attention to the extent of child prostitution in Victorian London – although it is of interest that this campaigning zeal did not extend to incest, which did not become a crime until 1908 – again reflecting differences between private and public spheres to which we have drawn attention. After the Act was passed a National Vigilance Association was established to ensure that requirements under the Act were implemented, and vigilance committees started to patrol areas of the city calling for the closure of brothels and lodging houses – all of which was given greater prominence with the murders of a number of prostitutes attributed to Jack the Ripper, which began in 1888.

Thomas (2000: 8) has argued that the age of consent is "gender specific and socially constructed", and we can see something of these issues in the debate that has taken place about lowering the age of consent for homosexuals. The age of consent for homosexual activity was first fixed at twenty-one by the Sexual Offences Act of 1967, but this was not established in Scottish law until 1980 and in Northern Ireland until 1982. The Criminal Justice and Public Order Act of 1994 lowered the age of consent to eighteen for all parts of the United Kingdom but – in response to a case brought by Euan Sutherland and Chris Morris – the European Court of Human Rights ruled that British law contravened the European Convention on Human Rights, given that the age of consent for heterosexuals was lower than the age of consent for homosexuals.

New Labour attempted to change the law on this matter by inserting a clause in the Crime and Disorder Bill of 1998 lowering the age of consent for homosexual activity to sixteen. However, this failed to pass the House of Lords, and subsequently failed again when a similar clause was introduced into the Sexual Offences (Amendment) Bill of the same year. They finally succeeded in lowering the age of consent to sixteen by invoking the Parliament Act in December 2000, thus establishing equality between homosexuals and heterosexuals. But whether or not we are dealing with homosexual or heterosexual activity, Donald West has raised another issue in relation to an age of consent. For example he points out that:

> The law maintains that no person under sixteen can give valid consent to a sexual act, so any sexual fondling of children below that age, however eager the children may have been to participate, amounts to an indecent assault. If two youngsters under sixteen indulge in petting, each is guilty of an assault upon the other. This is an example of legal overkill, for few could have passed through adolescence without having indulged in some petting, thereby putting themselves into the category of sex criminal. (West, 1987: 5)

Thus, as West reminds us, the "age" at which sexual activity begins, as far as the law is concerned, is not necessarily the age at which sex begins in practice – although ironically children are held to be criminally responsible from the age of ten in England and Wales, and at the age of eight in Scotland. And, while the law does give some scope for discretion when young people are just below the age of consent and the defendant just above, clearly there are still difficult issues which need to be raised. For example, when a doctor or nurse gives advice about contraception to a girl – or if they prescribe the pill – even though they know that the girl is below the age of consent, they do so in the knowledge that they may be enabling that girl to permit someone to commit the crime of unlawful sexual intercourse.

Thus on the one hand the age of consent attempts to protect children from being sexually exploited, but on the other hand – if enforced to the strict letter of the law – could in some circumstances prevent information about sexual activity being disseminated, at a time when it is likely that children will be sexually active and curious. How should we strike a balance here? Do we give information about, for example, "safe sex", condoms and the "morning after pill" to thirteen-, fourteen- and fifteen-year-olds, or do we ignore the reality of teenage pregnancies? And, if we accept that children younger than the age of consent are likely to be sexually active, is it right that we should allow companies to market products which aim to capitalize on this fact? Perhaps many would baulk at girls' magazines advising their readers on how to give "better blow jobs", but what about magazines that are aimed at the pre-teen and teenage market, which advise girls about fashion, make-up and relationships? The magazine *Mad About Boys*, for example, produced by Planet Three Publishing Network Ltd., encourages its readers to vote for a "Boy of the Month", and as the editorial in its third issue made clear:

> Time flies when you're looking at loadsa gorgeous boys all day long (tough job, eh?)! And take it from me – this month they ARE gorgeous AND we've got our first Boy of the Month as voted by you lot . . . let me tell you what else we've squashed into this issue – there's truly gorgeous covergirl makeover, fashion ideas that are fantastic for not-so-ladylike laydeez, [and] a quiz that'll make you REALLY think about where your loyalties lie . . . Happy choc-licious Easter, chicksters! (*Mad About Boys*, April 2001)

Is this harmless fun, or does it contribute to the pressures on young girls to be "adult", with all that that entails? What does it tell us about young boys, and this editor's interest in them? Indeed perhaps anxieties about some of these more general questions about child sexuality suggest, as with the moral panics about ticket of leave men and Mods and Rockers, a reason as to why we have chosen to be so censorious about the activities of paedophiles – at least with them we can be certain. This is a theme that we develop more fully throughout the book.

Another way of looking at "consent" is not to see this in relation to age, but, as with "informed consent", to view it as something which implies permission – based on the person giving that consent being fully aware of the facts and the consequences of its being given. (The term "consenting adults" suggests this dimension, for example.) If consent is not given – as in the crime of rape – then we move into the territory of sexual offending. Indeed, consent in this respect can be invalidated if, for example, the victim was scared, under duress or coerced into giving consent. However, this too becomes more complicated when we consider prostitution, which supposedly allows for sexual activity to take place in return for money, despite the fact that many feminist authors would point out that, in this respect, true consent has not been given as it is merely a function of poverty and inequality. Similarly, in the "Spanner" case of 1990, which involved a group of consenting homosexual men who were interested in sado-masochism, issues of consent did not prevent a successful prosecution of causing actual bodily harm; their convictions have been upheld on appeal and before the European Court of Human Rights.

We have spent some time on this issues of consent as it seems to us to be central to the issue of sexual offending, and while we have deliberately introduced ambiguity about consent this has been done to remind us of the complexity of the discussion that needs to be held, rather than relying on "common sense" assumptions. The final – and perhaps most important – ambiguity in all of this concerns the question: is child sex offending on the increase? Here of course we have to remember that, if "crime" can be invented or abolished, it is difficult to be precise about what it is that we are attempting to measure over any great period of time. And, in relation to sexual offending, there are other problems about using official statistics produced by the police. It is well known that some victims of sexual offences do not want to tell the police, for fear of not being taken seriously or of being subjected to intensive questioning and intrusive medical examinations. If this is true of adults (both female and male victims) it is clearly an even weightier factor in the case of children. Thus there is inevitably an under-reporting of sexual offences. Nonetheless, while these reservations should be borne in mind, recorded crime statistics do at least provide us with a starting-point from which to consider the overall level of child sexual offending within this country – an issue we discuss next.

Sex crime – the "facts"

The murder of eight-year-old Sarah Payne in the summer of 2000, which in many ways was the starting-point for this book, provoked an understandable bout of national soul-searching about paedophile offending. Callers to radio phone-ins, and writers of letters and emails to newspapers, overwhelmingly articulated the view that violent paedophile crime was getting out of hand, and that the failure to address it by government was a disgrace. Starting with the most extreme end of the spectrum – the murder of children with a sexual motive or element – there is no statistical support for this belief. Both Home Office figures and the Derbyshire police database called CATCHEM – which records all British cases – indicate that the number of child sex murders, where the perpetrator was a stranger, has remained roughly static, at between five and seven a year since about 1970. But what about the data for other sexual offences against children, short of killing?

As we have suggested, this is an area where the statistics have as much capacity to mislead as to illuminate. For example, the number of cautions or convictions for child-sex crimes has declined steadily in recent years. Home Office figures quoted by the distinguished forensic psychiatrist Don Grubin (1998) show that, in 1995, 3530 people were either convicted or cautioned in England and Wales for the six most common sexual offences against children under sixteen. The comparable figure for 1985 was 5136, a drop of 31 per cent. It is stretching credulity to believe that, during that decade, the real amount of sex crime against children dropped by almost a third, so we must look elsewhere for explanations – principally in variations in record-keeping from one police force to another; the withdrawal or downgrading of charges for evidential reasons; and the number of allegations dealt with other than through the criminal justice process.

Grubin (1998) notes that "with increased awareness and media interest in child sexual abuse, has come an increase in the number of reported cases in the UK." But criminologists disagree about whether this reflects a real rise in the incidence of abuse. Home Office research on offenders (Marshall, 1997) looked at cohorts of men born in 1953, 1958, 1963, 1968 and 1973, with a follow-up period to 1993. About 0.55 per cent of the 1953 and 1958 cohorts had a conviction for a sex offence against a child by the time they were thirty, compared with 0.45 per cent of the 1963 cohort, while the younger two cohorts seemed to be gathering sex offence convictions at an even slower rate. He estimated that 110,000 men in England and Wales had at least one conviction for a sexual offence against a child.

However, a number of victim surveys record a much higher proportion of child sex abuse in the general population than is implied by the Marshall findings. Baker and Duncan (1985), in conjunction with the opinion pollsters MORI, carried out one of the first national surveys, and from their findings extrapolated that over 4.5 million adults had been sexually abused as children, and that over 1.1 million children would be sexually abused by the age of fifteen. In 1992, the Department of Health estimated, from the number of children on child protection registers in respect of sexual abuse, that the incidence of such abuse in the UK was 0.6 per cent per 1000 girls and 0.2 per cent per 1000 boys. The latest Home Office criminal statistics available at the time of writing show child sex offences representing 7 per cent of the 37,300 sex crimes recorded by the police in England and Wales in the year ending March 2001. The largest categories were gross indecency with a child – 1336 – and illegal sex with a girl under sixteen – 1237; 155 people were convicted of having sex with a girl under thirteen.

Having studied all the relevant data available at the time of his study, Grubin comes to a startling conclusion, which helps to put much of the argument discussed in this book in perspective: that the number of children sexually abused each year in England and Wales lies somewhere between 3500 and 72,600. In other words, a detailed analysis of the statistics produces such a wide margin of possible error that no published figures can provide the basis for reliable assumptions, let alone sensible policy-making. Thus the belief (held by the *News of the World* and others) that, by focusing on one narrow measure of sexual crime, the Sex Offender Register, we are contributing to child protection is ludicrously wrong-headed.

Yet we can say with certainty that, as a society, we are undeniably more concerned about paedophile crime than we were twenty or

Table 1.3   Articles mentioning the words
paedophile/paedophilia, 1992–1998

Year	Guardian	Indep'ent	Telegraph	Mirror	Mail	Times
1992–5	254	254	309	267	60	168
1996	250	257	288	206	123	178
1997	252	280	219	209	222	236
Jan.–April						
1998	112	113	132	80	126	149
Total	868	904	948	765	531	731

even ten years ago. Taking the media as a barometer, Keith Soothill has been able to show that there has been "an explosion of interest" among the six leading British newspapers about paedophiles since 1996 (Soothill et al., 1998: 882; see also Soothill and Walby, 1991). A computer search of *The Guardian*, *The Independent*, the *Daily Telegraph*, the *Daily Mirror*, the *Daily Mail* and *The Times* for the words "paedophile" or "paedophilia" revealed, for example, that the *Daily Mail* had only sixty articles between 1992 and 1995 which mentioned these words, but had over double that number of articles in 1996 alone, and double that number again in 1997. Indeed in only the first four months of 1998, when Soothill did his search, the *Daily Mail* produced more than double the number of articles using these words than they had during the entire four years between 1992 and 1995. This was a pattern that was roughly consistent for the other tabloid newspaper – the *Daily Mirror* – although its interest in paedophiles seems to have peaked in 1997. Of the broadsheets, *The Guardian*, for example, had 254 articles that mentioned "paedophiles" or "paedophilia" in the four years between 1992 and 1995, but the same number of articles in 1996 alone, and the broadsheet with the greatest interest in paedophiles is the *Daily Telegraph*. The full breakdown of Soothill's findings is presented in table 1.3, and we discuss the impact of the *News of the World*'s "naming and shaming" campaign in chapter 8. However, as table 1.3 makes very clear, the media has played a crucial role in providing information about paedophiles and has contributed to creating a "moral panic" at a time when the numbers of sex offenders were actually stable within the sentenced prison population.

Responses to paedophiles and sexual offending

Whether or not the numbers of people being sentenced for sexual offences is stable, increasing or falling off, we do not intend to suggest that these offences are not serious – especially to those who experience them. All offending should be taken seriously, and each victim has a story to tell – an issue we explore in chapter 3. In this final section we present how the government has responded to the threats posed by sexual offenders within the community, and in particular we discuss the impact of the Sex Offenders Act 1997 – which introduced the Sex Offender Register and Sex Offender Orders, which were implemented on 1 December 1998 as part of the Crime and Disorder Act.

The Sex Offenders Act (SOA) received royal assent on 21 March 1997, just weeks before the general election, following a very short period of discussion both within and outside of Parliament. It was rushed through the Commons with cross-party support from the Labour opposition, in much the same way that Labour had supported the Crime (Sentences) Bill, a Tory initiative to introduce mandatory minimum sentencing, which became law after the election under a Labour administration. It was a period which was characterized by New Labour being determined not to be "out-toughened" on law and order by the Tories, which created a consensus between the two main parties, and it was left to the former Tory MP Matthew Parris – now a political columnist – to comment about the Sex Offenders Bill that "there is no reason for this Bill. No reason at all. It is simply a piece of electioneering" (*The Times*, 24 January 1997).

Nonetheless the SOA did have a slightly longer history than this would suggest, and Thomas (2000: 106) points out that, as long ago as 1988, the British Association of Social Workers had proposed a register of sex offenders, and that informal registers were being kept by some local authorities. Indeed the SOA itself came out of a Home Office consultation document on the sentencing and supervision of sex offenders (Home Office, 1996), and the idea of sex offender registration had support within the Police Superintendents' Association. Also of note, a paedophile section had been created within the National Criminal Intelligence Service.

The Sex Offenders Bill had been premised on the idea that sex offender registration would help police identify suspects after a crime had been committed; that it would help to prevent crime; and, finally, that it might act as a deterrent – issues that were all first explained within the consultation document. The Bill itself was published in two parts. Part 1 was concerned with registration arrangements, and Part 2 with what had become known as "sex tourism". In relation to this first part the Bill had five clauses, which related to:

- those who would have to register and for how long
- the information that had to be supplied
- making failure to supply that information an offence
- the position of young offenders
- empowering the courts to issue certificates stating details of a court hearing.

There were several differences between what had been proposed within the consultation document and the published Bill. For example, the number of offences which would require registration was reduced from thirty-two to fourteen, and thus, while in the consultation document those convicted of bigamy, soliciting a man and incest by a woman were required to register, under the provisions of the Bill they were not. More importantly, while the consultation document had been focused on England and Wales, the Bill was aimed at the whole of the United Kingdom, and thus extra lists of new qualifying offences were introduced to satisfy Scottish law and the law of Northern Ireland. As such Thomas (2000: 109–10) points out that, since the age of criminal responsibility in Scotland is eight, technically registration could take place from that age, despite the fact that a child involved in the same activity in England would not be regarded as having offended at all.

In relation to the debate that did take place within the Commons, three issues emerged which are perhaps still of relevance. Firstly the SOA was not to be retrospective. In other words, the requirement to register related only to those sex offenders who were currently in contact with the criminal justice system. In turn, as is implied by the idea of an "offenders" register, those who are not "offenders", because they have not been reported, caught or prosecuted, would not have to register, although those who were cautioned for a sexual offence would be required to do so. This latter requirement was yet another change between the consultation document and the published Bill. Finally, what was to happen to the information that the police had gathered? In short, what were the police to do with the register so that it actually protected the public? Were they obliged to disseminate the information to relevant bodies, and were the public to have access to the information?

This idea of "community notification" is not simply associated with the SOA, but had occurred as a result of other events during 1997 and the relentless reporting about paedophiles that we have discussed above. For example, in the summer of 1997 the North Wales Police had disclosed information to the local community about two ex-sex offenders, and these two in turn sought a judicial review of the police's decision. In July the High Court (R v. *Chief Constable of North Wales Police*, ex p. AB and CD) held that, although there is a general presumption that the police should not disclose information about offenders to third parties, they could do so in order to prevent crime or to alert the public to a perceived danger. The court ruled that, while blanket disclosures were objectionable, any decision to disclose information which was made in good faith, and on the careful consideration of the facts of the case and the risk of future offending, would not contravene Article 8 of the European Convention on Human Rights (right to respect for privacy and family life). The Court of Appeal eventually upheld this decision.

Decisions such as this provided some of the legal footing for the SOA, which now applies to all of those convicted or cautioned of an offence as outlined in Schedule 1 of the Act (see table 1.4). The

Table 1.4   Schedule 1: sexual offences to which Part I applies, offences in England and Wales

- Rape
- Intercourse with a girl under thirteen
- Intercourse with a girl between thirteen and sixteen
- Incest by a man
- Buggery
- Indecency between men
- Indecent assault on a woman
- Indecent assault on a man
- Assault with intent to commit buggery
- Causing or encouraging prostitution of, intercourse with, or indecent assault on a girl under sixteen
- Indecent conduct towards a young child
- Inciting a girl under sixteen to have incestuous sexual intercourse
- Taking indecent photographs of children
- Possession of indecent photographs of children

Act applies across the United Kingdom, and therefore Schedule 1 is subdivided into the law of England and Wales, the law in Scotland and the law in Northern Ireland. Section 2 of the Act sets out the details that are necessary when registration takes place, which can be given in person by the offender or in writing. A failure to comply with these requirements can result in a fine of up to £5000 and/or a period of imprisonment for up to six months. The Act also specifies how long an offender is required to register: thus, for example, someone sentenced to life imprisonment has to register indefinitely, while those given a sentence of six months or less must register for seven years. Those who are cautioned must register for five years.

One of the continuing debates about the SOA was the question of whether or not registration would be "retrospective" – an issue raised during parliamentary discussion about the Bill. The Home Office responded with a consultation document which proposed that there should be a civil order called the Community Protection Order. This was an attempt to allay fears that "unregistered" sex offenders who might be at large within the community would be able to avoid the requirement to register if they had not been in contact with the criminal justice system at the time that the SOA became law, on 1 September 1997. The Community Notification Order would be "triggered" if a person acted suspiciously, for example, outside a school, and the police knew that this person had a previous conviction for a sexual offence. In these circumstances the police could make an application to the court for a Community Protection Order, which would not only require the person to register but also lay down areas of the community which could not be entered.

The Community Protection Order was renamed the Sex Offender Order in the Crime and Disorder Act, and came into force on 1 December 1998. Orders last for at least five years and can be indefinite, and application for an order depends on the police's assessment of the risk that the offender poses to the community – thus using the ruling in the case brought against the North Wales Police. The Greater Manchester Police are reported to have been the first to have used such an order, when a man with convictions for rape committed after breaking into students' flats had once again been seen loitering around student accommodation in the city. The Sex Offender Order required this man to stay out of the southern part of the city between 10 p.m. and 7 a.m. for eight years (*The Independent*, 24 December 1998).

Conclusion

This chapter has been concerned with providing some overall context within which to understand our contemporary approaches to sex offenders and paedophiles. As such it has used the concept of "consent" to discuss what it is that we mean by "sexual offending", and has attempted to explain what we describe as changes in crime over time and between cultures. In relation to this we have used the theoretical concepts of deviancy amplification and moral panic. As such we have sought to explain how sometimes the best of intentions can have some unexpected consequences – often making the problem worse rather than better. In doing so we have looked at our historic desire to register offenders and provided the historical example of the garrotting panic of the 1860s, which saw released offenders – the ticket of leave men – having to be registered throughout the latter part of the Victorian period as a result of the Penal Servitude Act and the Habitual Criminals Act. We have used this historic example to cast some light on the Sex Offenders Act, which introduced the Sex Offender Register, and we have described the media's "discovery" of sex offenders. We have suggested that the media's interest in sex offenders has in the main been unhelpful, fuelling a moral panic and leading to demands for "community notification". Our next chapter looks more closely at one particular type of sex offender – the paedophile.

2
Paedophiles

One day in 1867, a farm hand from the village of Lapcourt, who was somewhat simple-minded, employed here then there, depending on the season, living hand-to-mouth from a little charity or in exchange for the worst sort of labor, sleeping in barns and stables, was turned in to the authorities. At the border of a field, he had obtained a few caresses from a little girl, just as he had done before and seen done by the village urchins round about him; for, at the edge of the wood, or in the ditch by the road leading to Saint Nicholas, they would play the familiar game called "curdled milk". So he was pointed out by the girl's parents to the mayor of the village, reported by the mayor to the gendarmes, led by the gendarmes to the judge, who indicted him and turned him over first to a doctor, then to two other experts who not only wrote their report but also had it published. What is the significant thing about this story? The pettiness of it all; the fact that this everyday occurrence in the life of village sexuality, these inconsequential bucolic pleasures, could become, from a certain time, the object not only of a collective intolerance but of a judicial action, a medical intervention, a careful clinical examination, and an entire theoretical elaboration.

Michel Foucault, The Will to Knowledge

In my town we all knew Red. He'd be around the streets and come to parties, and our parents would all say "Hi" – he was very much part of the community. Yet, we would never be allowed to play with Red on our own, even if he asked us to. It was just explained to us that we couldn't, and that if we did we'd be in trouble.

Robin Wilson, psychologist, Correctional Service of Canada

This chapter attempts to provide some basic information about paedophiles and their motivations. However, it also builds upon the information provided in the first chapter, which looked at offending in general and sexual offending in particular. Thus we have attempted to see "offending" and "crime" not as something that is fixed in concrete, but rather as something which responds to anxieties within society as a whole at particular points in time. As such we drew attention to the power possessed by a few in our community to label behaviours or acts as "crime". Indeed, in relation to paedophilia this is exactly what the French philosopher Michel Foucault is alluding to with his story of the farm hand in 1867, and how he was subsequently dealt with by the authorities. The question of why in 1867 this "everyday occurrence in the life of village sexuality" became of interest to the authorities echoes our own desire to answer why we have "discovered" the paedophile in the last few years, despite the fact that, like Red in Robin Wilson's childhood, they have always been part of our community. However, this chapter does not seek to provide a historical account of the various reactions to paedophilia in this country or elsewhere; instead it is concerned with the current state of knowledge about why some people are sexually interested in children, and what we might do about this. As a consequence we provide material culled from medical, psychological and criminological journals, but we also use the understanding that we have gained by talking to various experts about their work with paedophiles, both in this country and abroad. Finally we offer some tentative suggestions as to why we have "discovered" the paedophile in the last few years, and what we might do about that discovery.

Definitions

The new and comprehensive *Sage Dictionary of Criminology* has no entry for paedophilia, and we are instead obliged to look in textbooks aimed at psychiatrists to find our first definition of what paedophilia is, and who paedophiles are. Thus Paul Bebbington (1979: 265) advises that:

> Paedophilia is the condition of being erotically attracted to pre-pubertal children. Paedophiliacs fall into three groups: heterosexual,

29

homosexual, and indiscriminate. The last group is rarer and tends to be more disturbed. Paedophilic acts rarely involve violence or coercion and usually take the form of immature sex play such as looking, showing, kissing and fondling. Coitus is uncommon. Other deviations which may have child objects include sadomasochism and exhibitionism. There are three age-groups of adult participants: the adolescent (who may be looked upon as the upper end of a normal curve of immature sexual activity), the middle-aged and the elderly. The middle-aged group are mainly married, but with marital and social difficulties; the paedophilia may involve incest. The elderly paedophile is characterized by social isolation. Alcohol may be involved in releasing the behaviour in the latter two groups.

The adult partner is usually known to the child and in one study the child was an active participant in two-thirds of the cases. The age distribution of child partners is different for the two sexes. In boys, the distribution gradually phases into the curve for adult homosexual acts, but in girls it peaks at age seven to nine. This age frequency distribution parallels that for early sexual exploration in female children given by Kinsey, which reinforces the idea of child participation.

Management of the deviation includes proper and tactful handling of the turmoil aroused by a discovered paedophilic act and the protection of the child from that turmoil.

This definition, written nearly a quarter of a century ago, is helpful in several respects, if still falling short of something that is definitive and raising, in itself, other issues. Firstly, it is helpful in that it attempts to explain several themes that allow us to deconstruct the label "paedophile". Thus, for example, it is clear that there are various acts that can be described as paedophilic – from kissing, showing and looking to acts which involve violence and coercion, although Bebbington is quick to suggest that this is rare. The common factor in all of this is that the acts involve "pre-pubertal" children. The definition also introduces us to three groups who may be involved in paedophilia (although no gender is specified) – adolescents, the middle-aged (who are "mainly married") and the elderly. Other themes that emerge within this definition include incest, the social isolation experienced by paedophiles, and their "difficulties" and marital problems. Bebbington also raises the rarely mentioned issue of "child participation" and sexual experimentation, and finally describes how paedophiles might be managed.

Yet, as we have indicated, this definition can only take us so far. For example, by "pre-pubertal" Bebbington is obviously meaning to imply before the onset of puberty, but this does not necessarily specify an age range. Clearly the word "child" implies "young", but how young is young before we begin to see the act as deviant? Similarly, "adolescent" was one of the three "adult" groups identified by Bebbington. Yet, what age range does this imply, and should adolescents interested in other adolescents – who may or may not have reached puberty – be excluded from the definition? Nor is paedophilia seen as different from incest. Yet, for Mervin Glasser (1989: 1), a consultant psychiatrist and well-known expert on these matters, paedophilia is quite simply "child sexual abuse outside the family", and thus not incest at all. This is an important distinction, and we have constructed the book around a definition of abuse that takes place outside of the family, although clearly there have been times when issues related to incest have had to be accommodated.

The criminologist Donald West takes all of this one stage further. For example, he defines paedophilia as "significant erotic arousal on the part of a physically mature adult to pre-pubertal children or to a child in the early stages of pubertal development" (West 1987: 40). This is helpful, for, as the word "significant" implies, this is not a fleeting, sexual interest, but one that is more consistent and defined. Similarly, the phrase "physically mature adult" excludes adolescents who might be interested in each other – a problem which we raised with the Bebbington definition. West goes further than this, and also excluded from his definition is sexual attraction to physically developed adolescents, for "it is so widely experienced and acknowledged, through the pictures used in advertisements and 'soft porn' publications and the popularity of teenage prostitutes, that it scarcely amounts to deviance" (West, 1987: 40). Indeed West (1987: 45) suggests that adult–child sexual encounters are "common", and therefore "paedophile activity cannot always be attributed to a small amount of seriously pathological offenders, and the children involved cannot all be permanently damaged." Like Bebbington, West reports that paedophiles are likely to be socially shy, be unassertive, have low self-esteem and be insecure. Thus, "most paedophiles are gentle and tentative in their interactions with children, persuasive and seductive rather than coercive" (West, 1987: 50). We do not necessarily have to agree with this judgement – especially as it fails to accommodate how the victims of the paedophile might view this attention (see chapter 3) – but West does at least help us better to define what we mean when we use the label "paedophile" throughout this book. In short, we are describing sexual abuse, outside of the family, of pre-pubertal children by a physically mature adult,

Table 2.1 Paedophilia

Relationship	Gender	Developmental stage of victim	Sexual activity	Time	Age of offender
Family	Girls	Pubertal	Verbal suggestions	Transient	Youth
Step-family	Boys	Pre-pubertal	Fondling		Adult
Professional relationship			Penetration		
Stranger	Indiscriminate	Infants/babies	S & M	Fixated	Elderly

which in extreme cases is a deeply ingrained, life-long erotic prefer-ence. West does not describe the form that the abuse might take – beyond saying that coercion and violence is rare.

We will continue to return to these definitions to illustrate the text, and we present above a table of behaviours, issues and other factors that we have found helpful in thinking about paedophiles. Of note, table 2.1 was constructed in consultation with Wendy Leaver of the Toronto Sexual Abuse Squad, the work of which we describe in our conclusion. This table also helps us to identify more clearly those offenders with whom we are most concerned in the book, while at the same time reminding us what a diverse range of issues and behaviours the label "paedophilia" covers. Thus, for example, as we have inferred, we are not concerned with incest and are therefore not interested in those who sexually abuse within the family. Similarly, when thinking about the definitions we have already provided, and the characteristics associated with paedophiles, it is useful to think of the "bottom line" of table 2.1 as identifying the most dangerous paedophiles. This cannot be taken too far, for it is also clear, for example, that it does not matter to the victims of abuse if they have been abused by someone who is a youth or someone who is an elderly adult.

It might appear to some that these definitions are irrelevant, for "common sense" tells us that we all know what paedophilia is, that it "is wrong", and that we should all be concerned with the beha-viours that we have identified above. Yet, this is precisely why these definitions are important, for they help us better to identify which behaviours are "wrong" (and when they became defined as such), and who in particular we should be concerned with – in short, whom we should label "paedophile". In other cases they might help us to conclude that some behaviours, and some people, are not really worthy of our attention. Thus it is possible to conclude that, while all abuse is regrettable, there is clearly a world of difference between those who actively and regularly target babies and infants, who use violence or coercion to achieve their ends and have penetrative sex, and those who might have a passing interest in a pubertal youth, to whom they make an inappropriate suggestion. Indeed two of our most experienced therapists working with paedophiles – both of whom work at HMP Grendon (see below) – provide a glimpse of why these definitions and distinctions are important. Dr John Gordon, for example, a psychiatrist formerly in charge of G wing at the prison, which deals exclusively with a range of sex offenders, thinks that generally all "labels are unfortunate", and that specifically the label "paedophile" has been wrongly attributed to "fellas on the wing, who have to be called paedophiles, but in fact they are just not particularly pleasant towards children".

Julia Long, the psychologist in charge of running the prison's Sex Offender Treatment Programme (SOTP), takes this issue of labelling one stage further. Indeed, she states that labelling someone as a paedophile can "encourage offending". She went on to explain how this might happen, which echoes the idea of "deviancy amplification" that we introduced in our first chapter:

> My sense is that, if you repeatedly ask people to identify themselves as paedophiles, then that becomes their identity. I have seen that within treatment settings. When I was on the wing [see below] at Grendon there was pressure from all the other sex offenders to get everyone who had offended against a child to accept that they were paedophiles, whether that offender had offended against an eighteen-month-old baby or a fifteen-year-old girl. The more I thought about it over the years, the more I felt that insisting that somebody accepts that as their identity, time and time again it acts as a sort of risk factor. There must be lots of people outside that have fantasies about children, but who don't offend against them. Perhaps that's because their identity is so much more than simply being an offender. "I feel like offending against this girl, but I'm not going to because I'm a social worker, because I'm a father, because I'm so many other things that protect me from having to act out that fantasy." If all your identity is that you are a paedophile, that's your label – that's who you are first and foremost – then it's almost as if you have nothing to lose. You are going to be a paedophile whether you offend or don't offend.

Long is therefore keen not to assign labels at all, but she both acknowledges the ranges of behaviours that are now seen as being paedophilic and, within the context of penal culture, provides an interesting insight into a hierarchy of heinousness among paedophiles themselves. She explains that incest offenders, for example, are considered to be well down the pecking order, with other paedophiles shocked that someone could offend against their own children. Thus, "paedophiles who offend against children outside of the family consider themselves to be more worthy than offenders who offend against their own children."

In relation to those therapists to whom we talked at HMP Grendon, all described this range of behaviours accommodated within the label "paedophile", and, to a greater or lesser degree, each was concerned with the damage that inappropriate labelling caused. However, all recognized that paedophiles at the "extreme" end – or, as we have described it, at the "bottom line" of our table – were extremely dangerous and often violent people. When asked to estimate how many people were in this bottom line, Julia Long thought for a second, and then said: "well, I've been working with sex offenders for ten years, and I can count them, so I guess that tells you how rare they are. I've probably come across twenty in my time. I don't think that there are many in the system and, in terms of the extreme end – torturing, raping, killing – I think they are very rare." Similarly, while Jenny Stead, the probation officer seconded to work with the prisoners on G wing, can describe the extreme end of behaviours committed by paedophiles as "the violent predatory type, who'll suddenly go and abduct a child off the street and commit an assault of various sorts on them", she also admits; "I've never actually worked with anyone who has done that" – again reflecting how rare this type of behaviour is. Indeed, one former psychologist who worked at the prison, who did not wish to be identified, while acknowledging that even minor forms of sexual offending can be traumatic, is also keen to point out that:

> A lot of what passes as paedophilia does not involve physical harm to children. In fact some types of sexual offenders would be repulsed by the idea of physically harming a child. What's driving them is a sense of wanting to be close to a child inappropriately and wrongly, and in the process of achieving this harm might be caused to the child, which is terrible, but not necessarily posing a threat to the life of that child.

Explanations: a visit to HMP Grendon

This observation, that some paedophiles are merely wanting to establish a form of personal – albeit inappropriate – intimacy with a child, begins to open up a debate about the motivations of paedophiles. In short, why do they do what they do? Yet, before beginning to answer this question we should first take heed of West's observation that "there can be no firm answer to the causes of paedophilia", and that a variety of factors "in victims, situations, culture and sociobiology, as well as the personal history and psychodynamics of the individual and his sexual physiology, all need to be considered" (West, 1987: 74). Thus, West warns us not to attempt a global, all-encompassing, "one size fits all" explanation as to why people become sexually attracted towards children, which in any event would be further complicated by the range of behaviours that have been subsumed within the label "paedophile". Moreover, as West's conclusion implies, while some people might harbour sexual feelings towards children, they might never act upon those feelings unless they were sufficiently motivated to do so, with a suitable victim in a situation that allowed the abuse to take place.

These are important caveats, and they should be kept in mind when reading this section, which is dominated by our interviews with therapists working with paedophiles at HMP Grendon. HMP Grendon is a Category B prison (medium security) which was opened in 1963, and it is still the only prison in England and Wales to operate wholly as a therapeutic community. The prison is divided into five wings, each of which can accommodate some forty prisoners. The wings are based upon four key principles (c.f. Cullen, 1995):

- **Responsibility**: the regime encourages individual and collective responsibility, with each prisoner being obliged to take responsibility for their actions.
- **Empowerment**: every member of the community has a direct say in every aspect of how the prison is run, including a democratically held right to vote other prisoners out of therapy if they transgress against any of the three cardinal rules of therapy: no drink, no drugs and no violence.
- **Support**: the regime provides support from a variety of staff, including psychologists, psychiatrists, probation staff, educationalists and discipline staff – as well as from other inmates. This

support is invaluable, for prisoners are required to be open and honest about their problems and offending history, and have to feel safe to do so without fear of rejection, insult, abuse or attack.

- **Confrontation**: although it is important to provide an environment in which prisoners feel safe, a therapeutic community is also a place where there is direct and candid confrontation of those who attempt to minimize their offending, or the harm that they have caused to victims.

This would be hard enough to achieve in most penal environments, but the success of Grendon is that it operates as a therapeutic community with some very difficult offenders. Hobson and Shine (1998), for example, outline that, in 1994–5, of the 229 men that had been received into Grendon, 38 per cent had been convicted of violent offences; 28 per cent of robbery; 27 per cent of sexual offences; 4 per cent of dishonesty of some kind; and 3 per cent of arson. Bringing all of this closer to the present day, Shine and Newton (2000) describe the profile of receptions into the jail between 1995 and 2000 as "damaged, disturbed and dangerous"; three-quarters of their sample were serving determinate sentences, with an average sentence length of just under eight years, and a quarter were serving indeterminate (life) sentences, with a mean tariff of twelve years. Some 15 per cent of the sample were in prison for sexual offences.

Thus staff working at HMP Grendon have, as a result of the therapeutic nature of the regime, gained a unique insight into what it is that motivates offenders to behave as they do, and this includes all kinds of sex offenders, paedophiles among them. Of note, again as a result of the therapeutic regime, there is no separation of sexual offenders from other offenders, as would occur in almost every prison – and which we describe in chapter 4. Furthermore, the value of looking to Grendon for some explanations is underscored by the fact that a diverse group of staff works there – from educationalists, probation and prison officers, to psychologists and psychiatrists. As a result, within this one establishment is a range of professionals, each of whom has been trained within different cultures and traditions. This is no small matter, for it should be remembered that explanations of paedophilia range from psychoanalytical to sociological and cultural. Indeed, we structure the rest of this section around these themes, based on interviews conducted within the prison, but also alluding to other research where this is appropriate.

Psychoanalytical theory has tended to see any sexual behaviour – outside of a "traditional relationship" between a man and a woman – as an expression of an immaturity which is rooted in childhood trauma. Thus, generalizing very crudely, the person becomes a paedophile as a result of searching for a love object that most closely resembled that person as a child, at the point at which he experienced that trauma. As might be expected, Dr John Gordon, for example, believes that paedophilia is caused by the way people are "programmed . . . it depends on how people learn as they grow up". He amplifies this statement by explaining: "I think that they are people who have been abused by other men as children, and [thus] it has to do with how they react to particular experiences in their formative years." However, Dr Gordon also recognizes that all of this is not a simple, deterministic process, but, as "each individual has a set of experiences that are unique to him or to her", some who may have had similar abusive childhood experiences do not necessarily go on to abuse themselves. The process is thus more complicated, and he also acknowledges that some of these childhood experiences could be "good experiences". This seems to suggest not only that there are no simple answers, but also that it is difficult to generalize from these very unique circumstances in any broader theoretical way.

Nonetheless, this has not prevented many from attempting to do so. Thus, for example, Mervin Glasser (1989: 2) divides paedophilia into "primary" and "secondary" categories, with the latter occurring within the context of some other "pathology", such as schizophrenia and as a consequence of "ego-disintegration". On the other hand, "primary paedophilia" "is a perversion, sharing with other perversions a particular type of psychopathological structure which, amongst other things, enables the ego to sustain a relative degree of integration and stability". Glasser further divides primary paedophilia into "invariant" and "pseudo-neurotic" types. Thus the invariant paedophile is "an individual who is, and always has been, consistently involved with children and/or adolescents – boys more often than girls. He has no sexual (and often no social) interest in adults, male or female . . . [and] shows no real guilt or shame over his paedophilia." The pseudo-neurotic paedophile frequently presents, according to Glasser, as an individual with adult, heterosexual preferences, but suffers from "occasional impotence, perhaps a degree of sexual apathy and some tension and distress in his relationship between him and his partner". However, "at irregular intervals, apparently in response to a chance situation or to stressful happenings, he carries out a paedophilic act about which he professes great guilt or shame. But his inner world is really consistently paedophilic."

Glasser (1989: 7–10) goes on to suggest that there are special psychodynamic features related to paedophilia – in particular narcissism, and the relationship that paedophiles have to their superego. Thus, in relation to the former, "by identifying with the child he gives himself vicariously the gratification of the love and emotional recognition of which he bitterly feels he was deprived . . . his love is primarily self-gratifying." Interestingly, reflecting an observation made by Dr Gordon, Glasser believes that this helps us to "understand why it is that the age of the children to whom he is attracted is generally the age at which he was himself sexually molested". With regard to the paedophile's relationship with his superego – that part of our psychological make-up that is concerned with moral, ethical and idealistic issues, and which is formed during childhood – Glasser believes that this is "deceived" in the paedophile through "faulty development".

The important point to grasp from psychodynamic theories would seem to be that, while these have been developed on the basis of work with particular patients – which as we have suggested makes it difficult to generalize – childhood circumstances and development are central. Whether we accept or reject ideas related to narcissism or superego deception, what emerges from the literature is the importance of what happened to the paedophile in his childhood, which becomes internalized and prevents him from developing mature, adult relationships. However, other factors could be at work here also. Nor does psychoanalytical theory explain why some children who have been abused do not go on to abuse others – something that several therapists working at Grendon commented upon. For example, something frequently mentioned by those working with paedophiles, and included in the standard definitions of paedophilia that we provided at the start of this chapter, is that they may be also be shy, have poor social skills, or simply be ugly – all of which might conspire to work against their ability to form an adult relationship. And, of note, these issues are not psychodynamic or even sexual, but rather cultural and social, which does suggest that in our search for explanations we should not simply turn to psychiatrists.

Discovering the paedophile

Leaving aside questions of why paedophiles do what they do, the best place to observe the cultural and social factors which provide a context for our discussion of paedophilia is in relation to uncovering why we "discovered" the paedophile over the last few years. However, we are also keen to understand why it is that this discovery has paradoxically gone hand in glove with a growing and accepted sexualization of children in other spheres of contemporary life. Perhaps two unrelated incidents that were reported on while we were conducting our interviews at HMP Grendon serve to illustrate both the extent of the "discovery" of paedophilia and the anxiety that this discovery caused.

In March 2001 the Saatchi Gallery mounted an exhibition entitled "I am a Camera", and included a photograph that the artist Tierney Gearon took of her two children, then aged six and four, naked at a beach, except that both of them were wearing animal masks. The photograph caused uproar in the newspapers, and the gallery was subsequently raided by Scotland Yard's obscene publications unit. The *Daily Mail*'s editorial of 16 March – written after the Crown Prosecution Service decided that it would not after all prosecute the gallery – suggested that this was "encouraging evil". It went on: "what is at issue here isn't a celebration of childhood innocence . . . context is everything . . . masks and relentless nudity appear to hint at child abuse rituals. Whatever the intention behind the exhibition, it encourages all those paedophiles – who have never accepted that their perversion is wrong – to believe that their activities have the tacit sanction of the great and the good" (*Daily Mail*, 16 March 2001). Yet, all of this was further confused when *The Guardian* reported that an exhibition of 100 photographs taken by politicians in the House of Commons upper waiting room included Lord Healey's "Boy in Peking", which showed a small boy eating an ice cream with his penis hanging out of his trousers (*The Guardian*, 14 March 2001).

There were other related controversies reported on at this time, among them issues associated with air travel, when a male passenger claimed to have been "insulted" by new instructions introduced by one airline. Thus, on the same day as the *Daily Mail's* editorial about Tierney Gearon's photograph, *The Times* reported that British Airways had introduced new "child rules", which involved male

passengers being asked to move if they found themselves sitting next to an unaccompanied child. A spokesman for British Airways said: "flight crew and ticket staff were under instructions to keep men away from unaccompanied children wherever possible because of the dangers of paedophiles" (*The Times*, 16 March 2001).

These two incidents have not been chosen because they are in some way representative of the discovery of paedophiles, but rather simply because they were reported on during our visits to Grendon. Indeed it is the ubiquitous nature of reports of this kind that is of interest to us. For, while the Saatchi's exhibition was able to generate editorials in a range of newspapers and is a "strong" news story, as is obvious with *The Times*'s reporting of the in-flight rules at British Airways, the media is quite adept at finding new ways of explaining the "evil" of paedophilia and the cunning of paedophiles to seduce children. No place was safe for our children – not even in the sky; paedophiles were quite literally everywhere. And, as the *Daily Mail* seems to suggest, the "great and the good" – whoever they might be – seem to approve of paedophilic activity, which in turn implies that this situation will not change, unless of course the "less great and good" take matters into their own hands.

Yet, as we suggest, this discovery has taken place at a time when children have been sexualized in other spheres of public life, and not necessarily by paedophiles. The distinction between childhood and adulthood has become increasingly blurred, and as such – especially for girls – there is greater pressure on children from an earlier age to be "adult", with all that that entails. This was a paradox that we put to those therapists who were working with paedophiles at Grendon. Thus, Julia Long, for example, comments that she has "felt for some time that young children have been forced to grow up rather more quickly than is comfortable. I remember that when I was ten or twelve I was wearing party dresses, but it's not cool now for children to be wearing party dresses, and by ten they are already moving into short skirts and cotton tops and looking like their pop idols." She developed this answer by describing how children had become "commodities as well as consumers", and, as such, greetings cards which had children pose as adults in adult situations, music and fashion had all begun to use children in ways that she found disturbing. As she explained:

> It is not just the Saatchi exhibition, but rather the everyday images of children that are accepted as part of today's world. You can open any

magazine from *Jackie* to *Cosmopolitan* and all you see are images of very youthful women and children. It is difficult to tell these days if you are actually looking at a woman or a child . . . in *Jackie* you've got very sexualized images of children, which in turn encourages other children to wear make-up, short skirts, and to start behaving as if they are women by the age of nine or ten. Everyone latches on to the newspapers reporting breast implants for fourteen-year-olds, but what they don't latch onto is the more humdrum stuff. I guess I get cross when the Spice Girls dress up in school uniform. I don't think that anyone reacted to that because for quite some time the school uniform has been a sexy image, but for me that is exceptionally damaging.

This is not to imply that those we spoke with were happy with some of the photographs in the Saatchi exhibition. Jenny Stead, for example, found them "offensive", and thought that the photograph taken by Tierney Gearon "didn't seem to me to be a typical family photograph". She also suggested that some of the men that she was working with were upset by the photograph; that the photograph had echoed aspects of abuse in one offender's history, and that he "knows that there are photographs of him still circulating showing him wearing a mask". Similarly, one therapist admitted that he himself had complained about a book, some four years previously, which had shown children posing naked in a forest, and that he "knew for a fact that some paedophiles had access to this material".

However, all of the therapists – whatever their view about the Saatchi exhibition – recognized that, while paedophiles were being targeted as "icons of evil", the dangers for children did not come simply from paedophiles but also from broader cultural phenomena at work in society. Indeed, one therapist who wished to remain anonymous thought that "at the moment it's a bit of a scary place for a child to grow up", but that the causes of this were not simply about the presence of paedophiles. He explained: "It concerns me that there is this polarization of opinion, which on the one hand scapegoats paedophiles as the origins of society's evil, while at the same time, closer to home, there has been the sexualization of children in the media, fashion and the cosmetics industry." Indeed, he considered that it was important to "understand the links between these two seemingly unrelated phenomena, which I think are closely related".

The question of there being a relationship between these two phenomena cannot be tested empirically, but the likelihood that the two have a connection does at the very least suggest that children have a broad appeal to many adults who are not paedophiles, and who would frankly be offended by the suggestion. Nonetheless, dressing up small girls as adult women, or dressing adult women as small girls, is clearly working at a sexual level, whether we choose to acknowledge it or not. To deny that this is true obviously allows us to ignore some difficult questions about ourselves, and Julia Long "watched all the vilification of the paedophile in the community with great interest, because for me there's a sense in that vilification which allows us to deny responsibility for them, rather than seeing them as a product of our own society." For her, "our norms are what is going on, and what we've created." She remembered a conversation at a party, for example, when a male friend – knowing what she did at the jail – started to talk "very honestly about his own personal response to seeing two young girls of about ten and twelve, dressed as he saw it sexually and provocatively, and of being disturbed by his own response to them." For her this level of honesty was rare, for she found "that people get quite blinded whenever they start to talk about paedophiles."

Her use of the word "blinded" is of interest here, for, while it was prompted by a conversation with one individual man, it clearly also suggests something much broader about the community in which that man lived, and in which that conversation took place. It implies quite literally "not seeing" what it is that is happening in the community, and of denying the reality of who it is that is most likely to abuse children. Thus being blinded is not just a personal failure, but also a community failure, for the community refuses to accept responsibility for what it is that is happening in the community. But note, this is not some kind of "call to arms" on behalf of vigilantes – the "less great and good" – to take matters into their own hands; rather, it echoes the type of community that Robin Wilson described, where Red could be accommodated by everyone knowing and seeing who Red was, and what he was interested in; of controlling him through inclusion, rather than exclusion.

Yet, while all of this may be true, why has the paedophile been discovered now? One therapist, who did not want to be identified, provided clues as to why there has been a recent discovery of the paedophile. Although it did strike this therapist "as extremely odd" that this discovery had just happened, he attempted to construct an understanding of the forces at work. Thus, he thought:

Psychology plays a part in this to some extent. You are right – there have been people who have offended against children for a very long time, but until recently that was swept under the carpet. Unfortunately, a lot of our understanding had been to develop myths, and one of the greatest myths was perpetuated by Freud when his patients told him that they had been sexually abused as children. He said that that was fantasy . . . and generations then took this as fact, and we now know that Freud was wrong. In fact he was completely wrong, and this mistake emerged about twenty to twenty-five years ago, when the literature on child sexual abuse started to reveal a problem far greater than had been imagined. What happened was that there was a huge rethink about the whole problem, and we began to develop a much better understanding of the true level of the problem. I think that we are still working through that recognition.

So, in his understanding, the paedophile has been discovered as a result of the deconstruction of psychoanalytical theory, although this of course does not help to explain why it has occurred at the same time that we have chosen to sexualize children in the media, fashion or elsewhere. Nor does this explain why we collude with notions of "stranger danger", when in fact the psychoanalytical theory that was being described above related to sexual abuse within the home, rather than abuse by strangers. Perhaps the answer is far simpler, and Dr Gordon, for example, suggests that "people are particularly blind to the things that may have gone on in their own family – it is far easier to see abuse that's not quite so close to you" – yet another, albeit more personal, reference to being "blind".

An appropriate response

Given all that we have so far described, how should we respond to the reality of paedophiles in our community – to the "scary place" that our culture has become for children? Here we are concerned less with how paedophiles can be treated – a question that we address in chapter 4 – and more to see if community notification, or a British equivalent of "Megan's Law", will create a safer environment for our children – in short, to see if the sound and fury created by some sections of our media have been a help or a hindrance; after all a "common sense view" of the problem might see the public naming and shaming of paedophiles as contributing to a safer community.

Again, we addressed these questions to our Grendon therapists, and tried to contextualize their answers with those that they had previously given about why paedophiles became interested in children.

Thus, Julia Long explained that, having worked with paedophiles and understanding what was going on in their lives prior to their offending – which was usually "feeling very low, feeling very embittered, feeling very isolated, feeling very angry" – being "shamed" is something they begin to feel "quite comfortable with". More importantly, they use these feelings of exclusion and rejection "as permission to go on offending against children". She goes further, and suggests that "sticking their faces on posters and telling all the neighbours about where they are living" is "preposterous". She explained her position in the following way:

> I don't see that as being in any way helpful. It doesn't protect children in any way, shape or form that I can see. Quite apart from questions of logistics – how far and wide are you going to put these posters up? – you have to remember that paedophiles, like the rest of us, are more than capable of walking down the street and moving into another neighbourhood. They are more than capable of moving to an area where there have been no posters. I also think that this sets up the desire to offend; they feel low and angry and bitter, which is how I have characterized what was usually going on before they offended in the first place. I know that's what I would feel like if I was held to be an "undesirable" in the community, and my picture was posted on every lamppost and people were crossing the street to avoid me. I would feel lonely, angry and rejected and not owned by the community.

The other therapists echoed these themes. Thus, Jenny Stead, for example, was particularly critical of the *News of the World*'s campaign, which she described as "hysterical". She felt that "it is not looking at what does help make paedophiles more safe in the community", and that it specifically ignored the fact that most children were not abused by "strangers but by men in their own families". Furthermore, she thought that the campaign was driving paedophiles "underground", or having them running from place to place. Echoing comments made by Julia Long about this making the paedophile feel embittered and isolated – often factors that acted as accelerators to offending – she provided an example of someone that she was dealing with who had been community notified. "There was no chance for him in any sort of way to settle into the area", and as result he had run away to another area, where "he wasn't known and committed another offence". As far as she was concerned this was a crime that could have been prevented, for, "if he could have been allowed to settle in some sort of way in his original community, where he was known to the agencies, then it would have been quite different."

Dr Gordon thought that a British version of "Megan's Law" "would make no difference at all" to making the community safer for children, and while one therapist believed that there "was a role for close supervision and monitoring to protect the public", there had to be great care "that we do not stigmatize sex offenders and marginalize them to the extent where the risk of them reoffending is actually increased". When asked to explain how marginalizing paedophiles made them more likely to reoffend, he offered the following analysis:

> Imagine that offending has a cycle that builds up prior to offending. The person gives himself a sense of entitlement to offend; he has a sense of himself as a victim; he gets angry and cuts himself off from other people. He becomes a loner, and then starts to look for opportunities in which he can make contact with vulnerable people . . . marginalizing people seems to me to increase all those processes. You are going to increase the sense that paedophiles have that they are the victims; you are going to increase their sense of rejection – which is often a pattern which plays a part in their own offending. You are going to cut them off from key figures who might be able to give support and increase the likelihood that they will reoffend.

Thus, in one sense, what these therapists are suggesting goes far beyond a criticism of community notification, although their criticisms of this are trenchant and obvious. For, as they describe it, community notification can be seen as a failure of the community – an absence of community, rather than an expression of the community working together to manage the risks posed by paedophiles. Metaphorically, or in reality, putting up photographs of paedophiles, far from being a way to protect our children, actually increases the risks to our children, by increasing the stigmatization and exclusion of the paedophile. It precipitates an offending cycle that results in more children being abused. More importantly, in all of this we can see a way – at least theoretically – of managing paedophiles better, by acknowledging them as part of the community, and including them as such – like Robin Wilson's Red in his childhood, of accepting them as part of the world that we inhabit, and taking steps accordingly. This is a theme that we develop in our concluding chapter.

Conclusion

This chapter set out to provide some basic information about who paedophiles are and why they are motivated to do what they do. In doing so, it described a wide range of behaviours that have become subsumed within the label "paedophile", and, while all abuse is to be regretted, we suggested that some of the behaviours that are labelled as paedophilic are clearly less innocent than others. Indeed, we described how rare it is for paedophiles to be interested in harming children. We also suggested that, far from these less innocent behaviours being the sole preserve of paedophiles, there are many forces in our culture which use children sexually to sell music or fashion, and which clearly appeal to many adults who would never dream of calling themselves paedophiles.

Yet we also asked some broader theoretical questions. Namely, why is it that we "discovered" the paedophile at exactly the same time as this process of sexualizing our children seemed to gain pace? Similarly, we also wanted to know if community notification would actually make our community safer, and, if it wouldn't, why? In seeking answers to these questions we chose to interview a range of therapists working in the therapeutic community at HMP Grendon, who have unrivalled experience of working with paedophiles. As such they introduced us to ideas related to psychoanalytical theory and "offending cycles", and explained how being excluded, isolated and vilified – the process of community notification – were in fact often precursors to paedophiles' offending. In short, far from protecting the community, community notification was likely to make matters worse.

This chapter has therefore also been concerned with what we should do to make our community safer, if community notification is not the answer. And, while we did not develop this point fully (we leave this, as well as issues related to how paedophiles can be treated, to later chapters), we attempted to use the offending cycle of the paedophiles that was described to us to see if this could be better managed. Our starting-point was a comment by the Canadian psychologist Robin Wilson about Red, a paedophile in his community when he was growing up, and how Red was in effect managed by the community by his inclusion rather than by his exclusion. Thus we suggested "community notification", or a British version of "Megan's Law", are in fact failures of community. While they are clearly well-intentioned, they do little or nothing to bring the community together positively to solve a particular problem, but are rather driven by "blindness" – to borrow a word from one of our therapists. Yet in researching this chapter we have also reminded ourselves of the damage that paedophiles can do to young lives, and our intention has not been to minimize the risks that paedophiles can pose. As such our next chapter seeks to give voice to the victims of abuse.

3
Beyond Victimhood

When my children were growing up, sometimes I would look at them doing normal, happy things like playing and I used to think: "I can't remember doing anything like that as a child. I can't remember anything out of my childhood except horror." And that's really sad.

Lyn Costello

The title of this book, "Innocence Betrayed", was chosen with care. Look beneath the physiological impact of abuse, the lies and evasions practised by the abuser, the collusion, witting or unwitting, of others in the family or social circle, and you are left with the robbing of something uniquely precious – a child's freshly minted, untarnished outlook on the world. But although this is perhaps the most unforgivable violation of all – next to the taking of a life – the debate about paedophiles deserves better than the one-dimensional sermonizing which it often gets, where the abused are always "victims", the perpetrators "monsters". Like it or not, both are individuals and, though theirs is an unequal relationship, each may be looking for something – love or acceptance – which the other distorts, often with grotesque consequences.

This reality, far removed from the tabloid world of "stranger danger", is what we explore in this chapter through the eyes of two people. One is a woman who suffered both sexual and physical abuse as a child, though it is important to stress that she does not see herself as a victim nor, in therapy-speak, as a "survivor". Her story is illustrative of what happens inside a young girl's mind when the love and attention of adults comes at a price – the surrender of her body and her innocence. This is counter-balanced by the words of a convicted paedophile who traces his own deviancy to the events of his childhood. Their stories lend support to the view that there is such a thing as a cycle of abuse, passing from one generation to the next, though whether it is inevitable is a matter we make no judgement upon. We also use this chapter as a vehicle for a range of informed opinions which extend the paedophile debate beyond the narrow boundaries in which it invariably takes place.

Lyn's story

In April 1998, a group of women held a candle-lit vigil outside Wandsworth Prison in London. They were there to draw attention to the imminent release of one of the most notorious paedophiles of the last fifteen years, Sidney Cooke. Cooke, and two other men, Robert Oliver and Lennie Smith, were convicted in the late 1980s of the manslaughter of a fourteen-year-old boy, Jason Swift, during a drug-fuelled paedophile orgy in London. The Wandsworth Prison vigil was organized by a group called Mothers Against Murder, Manslaughter and Aggression (MAMMA), founded by two women as a response to the murder of James Bulger in 1993. Dee Warner and Lyn Costello have been in constant demand ever since to talk about violent crime. On this occasion, Lyn had a personal reason to be in front of the cameras because her own childhood was scarred by sexual abuse, not from a predatory paedophile like Cooke, but from members of her family – thus reinforcing one of our dominant themes, that sex offending has its most consistently damaging impact in the home. It is worth pointing out that Lyn, now forty-eight, has never told her story in public before.

She and her older sister, Sandy, had a tangled, turbulent childhood in which their principal carer was not their mother but their grandmother (who was forty-four when Lyn was born). The word "carer" is a misnomer because their grandmother, in Lyn's words, was "viciously cruel", a hypochondriac who would take to her bed for a week with an ingrowing toenail but not be too incapacitated to rise in a towering rage and mete out savage beatings with a belt. One of Lyn's earliest and most traumatic memories, at the age of about five (her sister was nearly seven), after some real or imagined misdemeanour, is of their grandmother packing two small suitcases and taking the girls to a nearby bus station, telling them they were to wait for their mother to come for them. They stayed there, alone, for two hours before their gran returned to collect them. The physical and emotional abuse went hand in hand:

> My gran was constantly putting us down. We were never good enough for her. And we were always being parcelled off to other members of the family to give her a break from us. I remember my uncle Vic – my mother's brother – coming out on weekend release from Dartmoor, and, that night, he got into bed with me and started touching me. He didn't hurt me, just touched me very gently, and I wasn't horrified or repelled by it at all. In fact, quite the opposite. The next day I said to my sister: "Uncle Vic loves me more than you because it was my bed he got into." My gran overheard and beat me black and blue. She said I'd asked for it (the touching-up) and I suppose it was true, because I was all over him like a rash, my arms constantly round his neck. You see, he showed me some attention – and nobody else did.

Another "uncle" also showed the girls attention over a number of years, and this is where Lyn's story takes on many of those universal elements which explain how paedophiles manage to get away with abuse even when those close to them are aware of what is happening.

Ronnie was the son of their gran's second husband. He was charming, extrovert, popular with all who knew him, a one-time singer, who would turn up on the doorstep with a beautiful woman on his arm and a sports car parked outside. He also abused both girls consistently. Lyn's sister, Sandy, said the first time with her was when she was three. Lyn says that she thought it started at about ten in her own case but accepts that it may well have been much younger. "Everybody loved Ronnie. He was literally the life and soul. And, to tell you the truth, he lit up our house when he came because our lives were so grim and repressed." It was the sixties, sexual liberation was sweeping away the cobwebbed conformism of the fifties and the girls were wearing mini-skirts. "I was developing breasts at the age of ten, eleven, and Ronnie would say things like: 'She's getting big in the chest.' And he'd be constantly touching us. He was quite open about it. But it was acceptable because it was Ronnie, the favourite son. And, you know, I loved him coming because he made me feel wanted."

Sexual abuse depends on not only the state of mind of the abuser – and, in Ronnie's case, it was fuelled by beer because he was an alcoholic – but opportunity. Some paedophiles spend many of their waking hours working out how they can be alone with their victim without arousing suspicion. Hence the willingness to babysit or the eagerness of the "serial boyfriend" to give their latest partner a break by taking the son or daughter away for the weekend. But, for Ronnie, opportunity was presented on a plate. With gran so frequently on her sickbed, Ronnie had the run of the house when he came to stay and would visit the girls in their bedrooms at night. At other times, he would suggest a drive in his latest high-performance car and caress them on the leather upholstery. "I didn't realize it was wrong. I just thought it was Ronnie's way, something he did. That's all."

When Lyn was eleven, the inevitable happened and Ronnie progressed from drink-induced petting to penetration. "The rape was terrible because it hurt so much and because I didn't have anyone to tell. In fact, that was worse than the physical pain. I was convinced that I was to blame for the rape by leading him on, and there was no way I was going to face another beating by telling my gran. Actually, it would have been worse than that. Ronnie was so popular that I would have been killed for having told." Despite these considerations, it was also impossible for a frightened and confused eleven-year-old not to confide in someone, and Lyn wrote a letter to her mother. "She immediately rang my gran and accused her of not looking after us properly. They had a right old row, but it didn't help me because I got beaten and I stayed with my gran. That night, I filled up the sink in my bedroom and shoved my face right in. I was going to drown myself because I couldn't believe the way my mother had betrayed me."

Even in the 1960s, before sexual abuse found its rightful place on the social agenda, there were potential external protectors – social workers, teachers, doctors – who sometimes picked up the warning signs and enabled interventions to be made. But then, as now, many children slipped through the net. In Lyn's case, it was because the family moved home so frequently:

> We never seemed to stay anywhere longer than a few months. I had about two years' schooling – and, to me, that's the worst form of abuse because I've got a good brain and I could have made something of myself. When I was ten, I had to have my appendix out, and I was ordered to tell the doctors that I was only eight to explain the gaps in my medical records. We just didn't come into contact with the kind of people who could have helped us. We weren't even allowed to play outside, ever, with other kids. I'm sure it was because my gran was scared we would tell them what was going on.

In common with other children who've suffered abuse, Lyn also acknowledges that, even if she and her sister had had regular schooling or other social contacts, they would probably have remained silent. "There are two reasons. We were so obedient and so conditioned that we wouldn't have dared say anything even if we had been given the opportunity. But, like many kids today, we just accepted what happened in our home as normal. I'll go further than that. I adored my grandmother. I used to lie awake at night and cry, thinking that, one day, she would die. Why did I cry about somebody who hurt me so badly and who let those things happen to me?"

Gerald

Gerald is thirty-six and was convicted just after his thirtieth birthday of indecently assaulting two young brothers aged eight and ten. The abuse had gone on consistently over two years. Gerald is about as different from the flamboyant Ronnie of Lyn's story as it is possible to be. He has a large soft body and a clammy handshake, and his pullover is flecked with dandruff. His eyes, behind heavy-rimmed spectacles, glance nervously at the floor or the walls of the room in which our interview takes place. You almost have the feeling that he wears an invisible sign around his neck saying: "I am a paedophile, beware." But because he has had intensive therapy, he talks readily and with insight about himself, and some of what he says echoes Lyn's words.

> Children who are abused tend not to say anything. I was abused by an uncle between the age of seven and eight and I said nothing because I was made somehow to feel partly responsible. So, in a way, you become complicit in the abuse, and the person doing it to you becomes almost like a friend. This is the pattern I have used myself. I gain the trust of families and then I use my position – I was a cub leader and ran the Boy's Brigade at the church – to become friends with the children. I could only "assault" a child with whom I had a relationship. I also made sure that the child had something to lose if he did tell. I took the two brothers on trips, such as to Euro Disney in Paris, so they had a vested interest in keeping quiet about what I was doing to them.

Lyn has not ventured a view on what made Ronnie – a man who was married five times and clearly enjoyed adult relationships – abuse children (though, presumably, the drink made it easier to rationalize). But it is well known that many paedophiles escape suspicion precisely because they are married or have a partner. Gerald, on the other hand, says that his view of himself and his sexuality was distorted irrevocably by the abuse at the hands of his uncle. "It had an almost immediate impact. From the age of eight or nine, I began to target other children, vulnerable kids, kids who were small for their age or were being bullied. I posed as their 'protector', and I was able to relate to them because I was bullied very badly at school so I knew what it felt like."

The legacy of abuse

The conventional wisdom is that the abused become abusers in their turn, though the nature of the link remains a matter of controversy. Whether they do or not, that sense of trust which we referred to at the beginning of this chapter, with which a child is naturally endowed, is broken. Henceforth, their world will have dark corners which will make it difficult, perhaps impossible, for them to forge relationships based on honesty and straightforwardness. Gerald turned his back on adults as a result of his childhood abuse:

> I just didn't feel that I could trust adults because I knew they would hurt me. So, as a substitute, I developed my meaningful relationships with children. I was happier, more comfortable with them. [This is known as emotional congruence: in other words, where there is a "fit" between the adult's emotional needs and the characteristics of the child/ren.] But my mind didn't stop working, and I knew, deep down, that what I was doing was wrong – more than that, it was illegal. That pushed my self-esteem down even further, and I made myself feel better the only way I knew how – by spending more time with children. It was a vicious cycle that I was trapped in.

Lyn's trust in adults, specifically men, was also shattered. But she found herself drawn to the kind of man, like Ronnie, who wanted only to use her. "I used to get incredibly drunk as a teenager, and sometimes I convinced myself that I had 'fuck me' written on my forehead. I couldn't have a platonic relationship with a man. I was just drawn to bastards who were going to use me and move on. After I was raped, I turned into a totally different person from this well-behaved obedient little girl I'd been. I became a lunatic for a while. I ran away, I was into drugs, cutting myself and drinking far too much." But she didn't abuse any of her own four children. "When the kids were small and I was in my twenties, I was always having breakdowns. I was permanently on anti-depressants, but even when I was totally drunk – and that was a lot of the time – I knew that I couldn't hurt them. I put my husbands through hell, and with my present one [Roger] I used to goad and provoke him mercilessly to see if he would beat me up. Just because I was conditioned to believe that that was what men did to me."

Destroying the myths

We have presented Lyn and Gerald's stories because, in their ordinariness, they make the point that child sexual abuse is not some kind of alien virus infecting the bloodstream of an otherwise healthy society and that, if we are serious about dealing with it, we have to look within ourselves. It follows therefore that talk of expelling paedophiles from communities is patently irrelevant. It also follows – and this is highly distasteful to many people – that, in order to make many paedophiles less harmful to children, they need to be seen as damaged rather than evil. One of the country's most experienced consultant psychiatrists, Dr Rob Hale, formerly of the Portman Clinic in London, puts it like this: "The paedophile remains a child even as an adult. And there is nearly always a 'victim within'. The sense of disenfranchisement and dislocation from one's peers begins at an early age. They are essentially loners and the treatment programme is very often the first time in their lives that they have been asked why they do it."

The problem, of course, is that this is as much a criminal justice issue as it is a psychosocial or health one, and the current obsession with paedophiles is focused not on how to treat them but how to punish them. Dr Hale believes a sensible society should see the two as inextricably linked:

> I am very concerned about the planned legislation dealing with those who have dangerous and severe personality disorders. It is all about

public protection because that is the easy political message to sell. The treatment side, which is the other side of the same coin, barely gets a mention. In the 1970s and 1980s, we, i.e. psychiatrists, would be asked to assess whether an offender needed treatment. Now, the courts often make that judgement themselves. The way our public policy is moving is making it harder and harder to look at why people become sex offenders.

Despite the fact that the most celebrated political catchphrase of the 1990s was Tony Blair's "Tough on crime, tough on the causes of crime", this is probably true. But then, as a society, we tend to have the rather curious notion that someone who does something as deviant as sex offending must have a completely different set of thought processes from the rest of us. Joe Sullivan, principal therapist at the Lucy Faithfull Foundation's Wolvercote Clinic in Epsom, the country's only residential institution for adult male sex offenders, says it's not so. "Sex offenders use 'cognitive distortion' to rationalize their behaviour, but that's only another term for 'mixed-up thinking', and we all do that to put ourselves in a better light or to minimize shameful things we may have done. So, when a Catholic priest who has abused children says: 'God accepts both parts of me, the bad as well as the good', he is only using the same kind of cognitive reasoning as we all do to justify our mistakes."

Put in this light, it can be seen that those who advocate the most extreme sanctions for paedophiles – such as castration – are missing the point as well as revealing something deeply disturbing about their own primitive urges. Sex offending is as much a function of the mind as of the body. It is as much about power as it is about lust. And there is no cure for it, only a set of strategies for controlling the urges and preventing the fantasies – which will almost certainly be life-long – from becoming reality.

It is our view that one of the underlying flaws in the current approach to paedophiles is what business consultants might call a failure to think "outside the box". In other words, in the search for better public protection, we have become so fixated on the Sex Offender Register and measures to restrict the movements of convicted paedophiles that we have lost sight of that vast number of people who abuse children and who never appear in any set of criminal justice statistics. It is true, as we said in chapter 1, that we have no accurate picture of the scale of child sex abuse in the UK but, from the number of children officially "at risk", it is evidently substantial. According to a Department of Health snapshot study, published in February 2000, more than 100,000 children in England and Wales were receiving care services because of abuse or neglect. Since most of their abusers will never be charged let alone convicted of any offence, what, at present, is happening to them? And is it in any way commensurate with the nature of the problem?

Ray Wyre has a long history in the field of advising on sexual crime. In the 1970s, he was a probation officer and then founded the Gracewell Institute for sex offenders in Birmingham. Now he is an independent consultant. Here is his analysis, which has been formed from his writing on the subject as well as from an interview with him undertaken for this book.

> This is what happens with an unconvicted sex offender. The social services will obtain a risk assessment, and the report might demonstrate that he is a risk to the children. They will inform him that, if he does not leave the home, they will remove the children into care. Usually, the person will leave the home. The very fact that he is being seen as a risk and is too dangerous to be in a home with the children suggests that just removing him is not about (general) child protection. However, if you suggest that the man should engage in a treatment programme, social services, in most areas, will say that he is not their responsibility. They have responsibility for the non-abusing partner and the child/ren. In any case, they do not have the resources to fund the offender in treatment. Although they *may* have protected the child/ren within the home, the man is likely to disappear, move area and join another family. If it is discovered, the whole process with social services will start again. There are clearly thousands of men in this position moving around the country, moving to different families, and no record is kept of them.

(These are the men whom the police describe as "serial boyfriends"). Ray Wyre's solution is this:

> I believe that social services should have responsibility for *all* children. They should not be offering a "child care plan" but a "child protection plan". It is important that, if a client is not convicted in the criminal courts, but is a risk to children, then he should still be given the opportunity for treatment. That is because moving him out of the home is not protecting anyone if he is motivated to abuse. He may not abduct a child. He doesn't need to, he can just join another family where he is not known.

As Ray Wyre points out, the problem at the moment is that the care agencies' safety net has gaping holes in it. Social services do not have the resources to send someone for treatment, even if they recognize his need for it. The probation service will say that they have no remit to work with him since he is unconvicted. And the mental health services will say he is not their problem because he is not mentally ill.

Craig Barlow, who was trained as a forensic social worker and is now an independent consultant in adult mental health, has also given much thought to this issue:

> What we need is a replica of the "Working Together" document following the Children Act. That signposted a multi-agency approach to children's matters. We need something similar for adult sex offenders and risk assessment. One of the key problems is the difficult relationship between social services and the NHS – "two services divided by a common language". Psychiatrists are very jealous about patient confidentiality. They are often reluctant to pass on information to other agencies because their primary concern is with the offender. In one sense, it is understandable because the patient/offender is their responsibility and, if anything goes wrong, they will be held to account. Sadly, no one is showing the same concern about the risk to the community. There are a few examples of good practice – Hertfordshire's Mental Health Services has set up a panel of senior health and social services managers, using the area child protection committee as a model – but there needs to be much more coordinated, centrally driven effort in this area.

In the myth-making about paedophilia, the most enduring cliché of all is the "dirty old man", usually found hanging around school playgrounds. Given that most offending takes place in the home and that as much as a third is committed by adolescents, this image is already well past its sell-by date. The reality, though, has many implications for the provision of services, not least because, in contrast to other forms of adolescent offending, sex offending is a behaviour that individuals grow into rather than out of. It is also true that sex offences are rarely "one-off" incidents but part of a trend which "tends to become more entrenched over time with patterns of increasing frequency and escalating seriousness not unusual" (Home Office, 1999).

In the light of this, it is clear that much more work needs to be done with school-age children to spot the signs of deviant behaviour early and, if necessary, intervene. As Craig Barlow points out: "If we catch them early enough in the cycle, the prognosis improves. This means going back way before the first conviction to early childhood, looking for signs like bed-wetting, cruelty to animals, crude arson attempts and so on. But, to do this successfully, we need to forge far stronger links between children's and adults' services in this country than we have at the moment." It should also be remembered that the very low detection rate for sexual offences means that it is rare that agencies have a full picture of an offender's behaviour on which to make assessments.

The cycle referred to by Craig Barlow is Wolf's Offending Cycle, a measure used by forensic psychologists to plot the route which can lead to paedophile behaviour. A typical pattern may go something like this. A man (most sex offenders are male, although female sex offending is by no means negligible) with a poor self-image is likely to be conditioned to expect rejection and failure. Each knock-back not only confirms the expectation but leads to the subject withdrawing into compensatory fantasies. These may begin in a non-sexual way – for example, what he imagines himself saying to his boss after being refused a pay rise – but they can progress to sexual fantasies and masturbation. Invariably, the fantasies are not an end in themselves but a rehearsal for acts, such as frequenting parks and playgrounds and swimming pools, "grooming" youngsters, and then minor offences like exposure. At that point, there may be strong feelings of guilt and shame, but they are overcome by the kind of cognitive distortion mentioned earlier, in which the act is rationalized. The extreme end of the spectrum is the rapist justifying his crime by saying "well, she was asking for it." (Gerald went through most of these stages.)

Craig Barlow: "The question is: how frequently does the cycle go round? And is the person missing out points on the cycle and accelerating his offending behaviour? This all gives a pointer to how dangerous he is likely to be." But one thing is certain, by the time the subject enters the criminal justice process – if, indeed he does – the cycle is already well in motion and may be unstoppable.

Ray Wyre calls this process a self-destruct course, in which the statutory authorities are, metaphorically, standing on the sidelines while the subject careers out of control. Occasionally, it ends with a man killing his family, or an even larger tragedy.

Take the case of Dunblane [the murder of sixteen children and their teacher in a school in the Scottish village of Dunblane in 1996 by Thomas Hamilton]. The media dealt only with the issue of guns – and of course, it led to legislation restricting gun use – but Hamilton was a case study in how our society fails to deal with the alleged child abuser in the community when he hasn't been before the law but is merely the subject of suspicion and innuendo. There were concerns about his behaviour with children for a number of years, and yet he was able to run groups and clubs without any kind of licensing or official supervision. Because of the failure of the statutory agencies, the community attempted to deal with it themselves. Hamilton was confronted and called a pervert, and the parents of the children in his youth club met and (rightly so) removed their children from the club. On a self-destruct course, he is likely to have said to himself: "If I can't have the children, no one else will." The lesson is that, unless we find ways of putting in place systems which recognize the needs and fears of the community, we will have more of these explosions as individuals feel they have no point in living.

Though the analysis may be correct, the prescription is fraught with difficulties – especially in an era of the Human Rights Act. After all, when the Lord Chief Justice, Lord Woolf, suggested in a radio interview (Radio 4, *Today*, 26 December 2001) that there might be a case for locking up some dangerous paedophiles before they had committed an offence (on the grounds that, once they had, it was self-evidently too late), the response was one of disbelief and anger in equal measure. Although the government is seriously considering some form of "civil detention" for people with a severe personality disorder who may pose a high risk, there are no plans to introduce something similar for those with no mental health problems.

"Stop it Now"

We have demonstrated that a system of child protection built around the criminal justice process is always going to be flawed. One of the reasons is that it seriously inhibits the reporting of sex crime. "What will happen if I tell someone in authority? What will they do to my dad/stepdad/brother etc? Will they go to jail?" These are questions which run inevitably through the minds of children who are being abused. There is also the fear – which, in many cases, becomes a reality – of the disclosure leading to an irrevocable rift with the mother, who may blame the traumatic disruption to "family" life on the abused rather than the abuser. Moreover, relying on criminal justice statistics alone gives a skewed impression about child sex abuse. Research for the Home Office estimates that roughly 15 to 17 per cent of those raped or indecently assaulted by a stranger report the crime, whereas the reporting rate for incest is about 2 per cent and the number of incest prosecutions is tiny. In 1997, for example, only twenty-five men and one woman were prosecuted at magistrates' courts in England and Wales on charges of incest. Yet we know that the number of people abused within the family dwarfs "stranger danger" (and may well lead to a more long-lasting trauma because of the breach of trust involved – *pace* Lyn's story).

In view of this, there must be more productive approaches than relying on the law. Or, put another way: "We should be asking a different question. Not, what does the public need from this process? But, what does the victim and his/her family need from it?" The speaker is Donald Findlater, manager at the Lucy Faithfull Foundation's Wolvercote Clinic and highly respected for his work with adult sex offenders. The foundation – along with Barnados, ChildLine, NSPCC and the National Organization for the Treatment of Offenders – is an advocate of an American programme called "Stop it Now", which was introduced in the UK during 2001. The idea is simple enough: that if child sex abuse is made a matter of public health education – like smoking or drinking and driving – it is possible to achieve quite dramatic shifts in social attitudes which have been entrenched for decades. The method is to run campaigns that reach adults rather than focus on child protection measures, which can be likened to a sticking plaster solution without tackling the cause of the malady. As Donald Findlater argues:

> The main point is to help people make that vital first step and seek help. It is absolutely appalling that, as a society, our knowledge of child sex abuse comes from the one in ten cases which get reported rather than the other nine which don't. Likewise, the resources are targeted at the 10 per cent rather than the 90 per cent. The term "child protection" itself is problematic because the only real work being done is when a child is being hit, or neglected or abused. We have little idea of what a "well" child looks like. If you think of it in

terms of drink-driving, it is like what happened a generation ago when people blithely got behind the wheel of a car when they were drunk because it was socially acceptable. The resources of the health service were being ploughed into dealing with the human damage rather than attacking the attitudes which encouraged it to happen. Now, a group going out to the pub or a restaurant will have a designated driver, and so on. There's been a sea change in attitudes. What we need is a preventative philosophy for child sex abuse and, over time, you will see attitudes change.

"Stop it Now" was born in 1995 in the fertile social climate of Vermont – fertile because it is a small, liberally inclined state (population about half a million) with a history of restorative justice and well-developed treatment programmes for convicted sex offenders, both inside and outside of prison. Naturally, those who inspired and nurtured "Stop it Now" are evangelistic about its potential, but we prefer to rely on evaluation data. Before the pilot programme was launched with a telephone helpline, pollsters asked a random sample of Vermonters whether they could explain the term "child sexual abuse". The number who said they could was 44.5 per cent. By 1999, after state-wide campaigns on radio and television and in newspapers, that figure had climbed to 84.8 per cent. The information about people calling the helpline is also striking in that 32 per cent were men, compared to an average of 10 per cent of male callers to other help services. The number of people who acknowledged that sexual abusers were living in their communities, and said they were prepared to take action to report it, had also gone up.

In 1999, the charismatic founder of "Stop it Now", Fran Henry, came to the UK to proselytize, and outlined four noteworthy developments in Vermont which have flowed from the programme in a keynote address to the conference of the National Organization for the Treatment of Offenders.

1   We have learned about gaps in the system which prevent people from coming forward – issues like learning to deny abuse while charges are pending – a denial which complicates getting help and treatment.
2   We have seen a significant shift in the attitudes of public officials, including the defender-general, the attorney-general, the corrections commissioner and head of human services in the state. Their initial views were cautious, but now we are able to count on their interest and enthusiasm for results.

3   We have witnessed a significant change in media attitudes, from viewing "Stop it Now" as only a helpline to understanding that child sexual abuse is a preventable public health problem. In the first year of the campaign, TV nightly news coverage went from an average of forty-five seconds to two minutes per story. The quality of the coverage has improved dramatically.

4   We have interested the US Centres for Disease Control and Prevention in evaluating our programmes. They are partnering us in Philadelphia to help us learn how this programme can be replicated elsewhere.

Although most of these gains – except the first – do not relate directly to the criminal justice system, there are benefits there too. A district attorney in one area of Vermont (Chittenden), who has compared data, found a much higher rate of guilty pleas to child sex charges in 2000 than five years previously. This is of relevance in the UK, where the anecdotal evidence is that a large number of alleged sex offenders plead not guilty, (a) hoping the evidence, particularly of victims, will fall short in court; (b) fearing draconian punishment; and (c) trusting in a jury to acquit – which, in more than half of such cases, they do. As Ray Wyre says, if something can be done to change the view that, in certain circumstances, you can commit child sex abuse with impunity, a breakthrough will have been achieved: "The conviction rate in the UK is abysmally low – something like 5 per cent. And abuse of under-fives is virtually immune from prosecution because of evidential difficulties. So, in the sense that most cases never get anywhere near a criminal court and, of those that do, the majority fail, you can say that sex offending against children in this country is virtually out of control."

Changing the law

Two threads have run in parallel through this chapter. One is that the vast majority of sexual offences against children are committed in settings where there is already some kind of relationship between the victim and perpetrator – quite frequently the home. We recognize that this is hardly a novel idea, but to anyone who gains their "understanding" of such matters from the mass media it might appear surprising. The second is that expecting the criminal justice process to deal with sex abuse says more about our obsession with punishment than it does about our knowledge of how to address a complex social phenomenon. Having said that, criminal justice clearly has a role to play, and there are ways in which it could be more effective.

In the summer of 2000, the Home Office published the results of a wide-ranging review of legislation on sex offences in England and Wales. *Setting the Boundaries: Reforming the Law on Sex Offences* is a valuable document which contains many sensible recommendations (as well as one or two which seem a trifle eccentric), but for our purposes the areas of interest are in chapter 3 ("Children") and chapter 5 ("Sexual Abuse within the Family"). The report recognizes that sexual abuse of children frequently takes place over a long period of time, but for the perpetrator to be prosecuted there have to be specific instances – dates, times, etc. – listed on the indictment. However, "by using such specific indictments, the court does not deal adequately with the pattern of abuse, especially the nature of organised and/or multiple abuse, nor does sentencing necessarily reflect that course of conduct which the specific charges were brought in to illustrate." The authors of the report recommend that an offence of *persistent sexual abuse* of a child should be introduced, to reflect a course of conduct which, if found proved, should attract a heavy sanction. It is a sound suggestion – though, as the report points out, in the Australian state of Victoria (where such an offence was introduced in 1991) it has been used only on a couple of occasions.

The other proposal which has merit concerns abuse within the family. As we noted earlier, the offence of incest is rarely prosecuted and, recognizing that the family of the twenty-first century is far looser and not bound together by blood relationships in the way that its predecessors were, it is clearly time to frame a law which is more contemporary in outlook. The report's solution is to replace the offence of incest with a new offence of *familial sexual abuse*, which can be applied not just to blood relatives who abuse children under eighteen but to anyone within the family structure in a position of responsibility or authority. To give this teeth, it is important that a parallel recommendation (no. 38 in the report) is also taken up, which would treat adoptive parents on the same basis as natural parents. We have stated a number of times our concerns about the "serial boyfriend". It is high time that the law reflected those concerns too.

Conclusion

There is a line in the *Setting the Boundaries* report which expresses concisely the philosophy that imbues much of this book – that all abuse is pernicious but abuse within the family is a double betrayal. "There is something very particular about the family – the place where we should all be safest – becoming the place of abuse and exploitation." But no report can adequately reflect the long-term trauma which individual family members, particularly siblings, suffer as a result of sustained abuse. Well into her adulthood, Lyn Costello was plagued by a question at the back of her mind:

> Why me and not my sister, Sandy? Why did the abuse happen to me and not her? You see, whenever I tried to talk to her, she refused to admit that Ronnie had abused her as well. It seemed that she'd had a completely different childhood from me. Then, when she was thirty-three, she had a nervous breakdown and she rang me out of the blue when I was at work, and she kept saying, over and over, "I'm so sorry, I'm so sorry." I said: "What are you sorry for?" And she just said: "All those years and I denied it, I denied everything."

If Sandy allowed her mind to blank out the horror, Lyn turned her mind to spinning a fantasy. "During the worst years, I had this imaginary figure who was going to save me – my father. I used to imagine that, when he found out what was happening to me, he would turn up at the door and kill them – my grandmother, my step-grandfather and Ronnie. Kill them all. The tragic thing is that the fantasy went on until I was in my twenties."

4
Dealing with Paedophiles within the Penal System

People don't really understand what we do. They know that we lock paedophiles up, but by and large we don't get good publicity. When you see how the TV portrays therapy being done in prison it's not particularly good, and some of these prison dramas are awful. I was quite mortified when I saw one recently, and wondered if that's what people actually thought that we did on the SOTP. Even my family passed comments to me – "Is that what you do?", they asked. It really isn't helpful the kind of publicity that we get.

Female principal officer in charge of the SOTP at HMP Wayland

This chapter is concerned with describing how HM Prison Service deals with paedophiles and other sex offenders. It is based on original research undertaken at HMP Wayland in Norfolk – a traditional Category C prison, which recently housed Lord Archer, where staff working with paedophiles, as well as the current governor of the prison, Kate Cawley, were interviewed. In particular we seek to describe the prison service's Sex Offender Treatment Programme (SOTP), and we provide some background to its introduction into the penal system as well as some criticisms of the programme. We also present a recent evaluation of the SOTP, which was particularly concerned with paedophiles. This chapter should be read in conjunction with chapter 2, which describes how sex offenders are managed within the specialist therapeutic community at HMP Grendon. However, what is presented here are the routines and practices that are found in the majority of closed prisons in this country, and as such this is meant to counter-balance the unique conditions that were encountered at HMP Grendon.

The Sex Offender Treatment Programme

The Sex Offender Treatment Programme (SOTP) was introduced into the prison service in the summer of 1991. Kenneth Baker (Home Office, 1991), home secretary at the time, explained the rationale behind the programme:

- Sex offenders would be held in fewer prisons to facilitate consistency of approach in running treatment programmes, to make cost-effective use of resources and skills, and to provide a safe and supportive environment.
- Treatment programmes would be based on an admission of offences, challenging attitudes and tackling offending behaviour. They would be practical, deliverable and sustainable and properly evaluated.
- Priority for treatment would be given to those who are likely to represent the greatest risk to the community on release.
- Assessment would be introduced following conviction and sentence to determine which prisoners are most in need of treatment. This assessment would take into account an inmate's previous convictions, evidence of inadequacy or addiction, evidence of sexual deviance, etc., and also reflect his behaviour during the assessment period, when he would undergo psychological tests, have individual counselling and participate in group work.
- Two main treatment programmes would be available in the prison service:

    A core programme, which does not require significant specialist resources, will tackle offenders' distorted beliefs about relationships, enhance their awareness of the effect of sexual offences on the victim, and seek to get inmates to take responsibility for and face up to the consequences of their own offending behaviour. The programme also gets inmates to develop relapse prevention strategies, and identify the nature of their offence cycles and how high risk strategies could be avoided.
    An extended programme, for those who represent the greatest risk, will be run at establishments with appropriate specialist resources. This will, in addition, tackle problems of deviant arousal, inter-personal relationships, communications skills, anger and stress management, and substance abuse.

These two programmes were subsequently introduced progressively, and by 1992 some twenty prisons were running the SOTP, including HMPs Albany, Dartmoor, Full Sutton, Maidstone, Wakefield, Wandsworth, Littlehey, Channings Wood, Featherstone, Risley, Usk, Whatton, Grendon, Wormwood Scrubs, Swinfen Hall and Wayland. Baker justified the introduction of these programmes on a number of factors. For example, he commented on the growth in the numbers of sex offenders being sent to prison (see chapter 1), and the fact that the Criminal Justice Act of 1991, which was about to be implemented, would put particular emphasis on tackling offending behaviour. Here, Baker's concern was with public safety: "the need to protect potential victims (rather than simply the benefit to the prisoner) is the paramount concern in the treatment and management of sex offenders" (Home Office, 1991). Finally, he made a rather oblique reference to the recently published Woolf Inquiry into the riots at HMP Strangeways and elsewhere during 1990, which had made some particularly scathing comments about how the prison service had handled sex offenders – largely through segregation from other prisoners under Rule 43 of the prison rules. Indeed Woolf had argued for a thorough overhaul of the Rule 43 system, which, because of the lack of regime provision for those on Rule 43 and the constant threats that they faced from other prisoners, had encouraged sex offenders to think of themselves as "victims". Indeed, arguments of this kind had been made repeatedly about Rule 43 by several of the penal pressure groups – including the Prison Reform Trust – in, for example their policy document *Sex Offenders in Prison* (1990), which had described the prison service's approach to sex offenders as "incoherent and unimaginative".

However, by far the greatest debt for the development of the SOTP was work being undertaken by psychologists in American and Canadian prisons, which has since been characterized as "cognitive behaviour therapy". While there is no single cognitive behavioural theory or method, and instead – as James McGuire (2000: 21) has described it – a "family" of methods, in essence cognitive behaviour therapy looks at the dynamic relationship between thoughts, feelings and behaviour. As such it is a conjunction of two different psychological traditions – behaviourism and cognitivism. From the former tradition comes a recognition of the importance of the environment; breaking down seemingly complex behaviour into simpler units, with the possibility of changing this behaviour over time, step by step; and the evaluation of the results. From the latter comes a focus on conscious experience; the importance of language; intro-spection; and the value of self-reports. Thus, in relation to offend-ers, cognitive behavioural approaches would focus on decision-making processes, self-esteem, self-statements and cognitive skills, but would not be "detached from other explanations of crime, but convergent with them at a whole series of points" (McGuire, 2000: 37). In short, it is not simply about an offender's individual or psychological make-up or "personality".

Perhaps the important point to grasp here is that, when attempt-ing to change the behaviour of offenders, cognitive behavioural approaches came to challenge the assumption that "nothing works". This view, perhaps unfairly associated with Robert Martinson (1974), concluded, on the basis of evidence from a wide range of studies undertaken with offenders to reduce their "offence-proneness", con-ducted in the United States and Britain, that there was no evidence that anything actually worked. This belief became the dominant view within criminal justice circles on both sides of the Atlantic, partly because it could be used to justify broader criminological aspirations for those at both ends of the political spectrum. For those on the left, for example, this form of "penal pessimism" could be used to argue against putting people in custody, and instead to develop and support community penalties. On the other hand, for those on the right, if "treatment" didn't work – thus making rehabilitation impossible – the goal of imprisonment should be pun-ishment (and the longer the better to deter others), and investment in programmes for prisoners could be cut.

However Blackburn (1980), and particularly Gendreau and Ross (1980) – who compiled a "bibliotherapy for cynics" in the form of a collection of articles which reported positive treatment results in work with offenders – and McGuire and Priestley (1985), set out to demonstrate that, in fact, "some things work". They worked even for sex offenders, and Eddie Guy (1992: 5), the civil servant in charge of introducing SOTP to the prison service, acknowledged that:

> The core programme is deliberately based on the cognitive behavioural programmes that have been found to be successful in Canada and the USA. It is now generally accepted that most sex offenders are not mentally ill and do not benefit from traditional psychiatric treatment. Sex offenders, like some other offender groups, employ distorted patterns of thinking that allow them to initiate and then rationalise their behaviour. These attitudes include the beliefs that children can

consent to sex with an adult, that fondling does not constitute sexual abuse, and that victims are responsible for being sexually assaulted.

And, writing from the vantage point of 2000, James McGuire (2000: 97) was able to describe how "it can be demonstrated that the net effect of 'treatment' in the many studies surveyed represents on average a reduction in recidivism of approximately ten percentage points. But in studies meeting certain additional criteria, this figure ranges between 20% and 30% and is in some cases even higher."

The SOTP in practice

HM Prison Service is an executive agency of the Home Office and has two main objectives:

- to protect the public by holding those committed by the courts in a safe, decent and healthy environment.
- to reduce crime by providing constructive regimes which address offending behaviour, improve educational and work skills and promote law-abiding behaviour in custody and after release.

Various key performance targets and indicators (KPIs) are set to measure the service's performance against these objectives. In relation to the latter, the KPI for 2001–2 was to "deliver 6,100 accredited offender behaviour completions . . . including 1,160 sex offender treatment programmes". Thus, the SOTP – which is currently run in some twenty-five prisons – is central to the success of the prison service in achieving what it claims to be concerned with, and a basis on how we should judge its performance.

As was initially conceptualized, but with a variety of minor adjustments, the SOTP is based on a core and an extended programme. The core programme is available to any male prisoner who is currently convicted of a sex offence who has time left in prison to complete the programme. In addition, offenders not currently convicted of a sexual offence, but with a history of previous sexual offending, are eligible for the core programme, as are prisoners convicted of serious violence where there is a sexual element. This eligibility is rather broader than was initially envisaged, and perhaps reflects criticisms from within the prison service when the proposals were originally announced, at a conference held at a seminar to introduce the programmes at Newbold Revel between 30 January and 1 February 1991 (Home Office, 1991). The extended programme is designed to tackle offenders who have difficulties with anger control, are unable to express feelings, and have problems in managing stress, alcohol or drug abuse and "deviant sexual arousal" (Guy, 1992: 5).

The two most important factors to take into account for selecting prisoners for the core programme are their level of risk and their date of release. As such there is a risk assessment completed on all prisoners convicted of a sexual offence, and those rated high or medium risk receive priority for treatment over those rated low risk. As the *Core Programme Manual* explains, this is because "research has clearly demonstrated that the programme is more effective with High Risk sex offenders" (Prison Service, 1996: 3), something which should be remembered when we discuss the evaluation of the programme (see below). The SOTP is also considered relevant to a life-sentenced prisoner who has committed an offence with a "sexual element". The *Core Programme Manual* explains that a sexual element can be regarded as being present if the offence included sexual abuse or assault, even if the actual conviction does not mention the sexual element – as in the case, for example, of a man who raped and murdered, but who is charged only with murder. Similarly, a sexual element can be regarded as being present if forensic evidence suggests that there were injuries to the victim's sexual organs, even if there is "no proof or admission of a sexual offence", or if there is a previous conviction for a sexual offence, or, finally, "when the offending manifested behavioural trends that might imply future sexual offending – e.g. murdering someone as a consequence of their refusing to have sex with him" (Prison Service, 1996: 3).

Prisoners can be excluded from the SOTP if they cannot speak English, have an IQ of less than 80, are mentally ill or are appealing against their conviction. However, those who are a suicide risk are excused only if they display "persistent acting-out self-injury", and would be made "materially worse by the stress of participating in the programme". Prisoners are not excluded from the programme if they deny their offence, if they claim that they cannot handle groupwork, or claim to be "cured" as a result of treatment elsewhere. The issue of denial is important, and is one to which we will return below. However, for the moment it is enough to acknowledge that

Table 4.1   The twenty SOTP blocks

1	Establishing the group	1 session
2	Introducing cognitive disorders	1 session
3	Introducing Finkelhor's preconditions	1 session
4	Brief offence accounts	4 sessions
5	Active accounts	24 sessions
6	Victim empathy – written accounts	1 session
7	Victim empathy – video	2 sessions
8	Victim narratives	4 sessions
9	Victim roleplays	8 sessions
6–9	Summary session	1 session
10	Consequences of offending	1 session
11	Decision chains	2 sessions
12	Individual chains	8 sessions
13	Individual alternatives	8 sessions
14	Risk factors	1 session
15	Recognizing common risk factors	1 session
16	Recognizing individual risk factors	4 sessions
17	Relapse prevention planning	9 sessions
18	Abstinence violation effects	1 session
19	Risk factors in prison	1 session
20	Reviewing the RP plans	2 sessions

the *Core Programme Manual* suggests that "sex offenders in total denial may need to be worked with separately or attend a special denial programme" (Prison Service, 1996: 4).

The core programme is divided into twenty blocks that make up a total of eighty-five sessions (see table 4.1). Block 3, for example, aims to give group members an understanding of Finkelhor's preconditions model, and then to get them to begin to map their own experience of sexual offending into Finkelhor's categories. Briefly, Finkelhor claims that for an offence to occur four steps must first be followed. These are:

- **Wanting to offend**: wanting to abuse because you have an emotional or sexual need to satisfy
- **Giving permission**: making excuses to yourself about how it would be OK to offend
- **Creating the opportunity**: setting up a situation in which you can offend

- **Overcoming victim resistance**: making the victim comply with your wishes (e.g. threatening, forcing, bribing).

A great deal is at stake for the offender to complete the core programme, even if the prison service rarely publicly acknowledges this. If, for example, he refused to participate, or failed to complete the programme, there would be various regime consequences – from access to fewer privileges to review of his security classification, and wider considerations related to, for instance, his suitability for parole. While it is difficult to get access to official information on this matter, it is clear from answers given at the Newbold Revel conference mentioned above, and printed in the conference proceedings, that a "carrot and stick" approach is being adopted. Thus, for example, while acknowledging that "all prisoners will have their own reasons for taking or not taking treatment – we all have our ulterior motives", the reality is that "if a prisoner thinks that early release on parole depends on treatment then he may see this as positive encouragement to participate", and "prisoners who opt out of treatment may be transferred off the wing" (Prison Service, 1996: 96). As we have written elsewhere (Wilson, 1999), this comes very close to what political philosophers describe as a "throffer" – the mixture of a threat with an offer. The "offer" is the treatment, with its promise of release, and the "threat" the failure to secure release – especially by gaining parole. This threat is quite explicit, despite the fact that the SOTP wants "volunteers" to engage in the programme. Thus, for example, Guy (1992: 5) explains that the programme will prioritize those with the longest sentence, as this reflects the seriousness of the offence, and the fact that "Such offenders will be subject to a selective system of parole. The extent to which their offending behaviour has been addressed in prison is likely to be an important factor in reaching that parole decision." It is thus quite clear that, to get parole, any sex offender would have to admit his guilt and participate in programmes to work on his offence, and his "cognitive distortions".

There are several difficulties here, especially if the offender is in fact innocent of the offence for which he was convicted. One prisoner, for example, wrote to the Prison Reform Trust (quoted in Wilson, 1999: 65–6) from HMP Risley about this predicament:

> I am currently serving a seven year sentence for alleged rape which
> I always maintain that I did not commit . . . I have settled into my

sentence in a peaceful manner, worked every day available and only had one adjudication upheld against me . . . 12 months ago I made enquiries with my personal officer about obtaining Category D status [this would have allowed this prisoner to move to an open prison]. I was advised by him to use the Request and Complaints procedure which I did, and have in my possession the reply stating the prison system will not consider me for Category D status without addressing my alleged "offending behaviour" . . . obviously I am of the opinion that this constitutes a rather vulgar form of blackmail, in that my refusal to lie, by taking part in the "core programme" and pretending that I did commit the offence, even though I didn't – which they would like me to do, gives them the right to say that I have no chance of being given parole, though this was not a condition imposed upon me at the time of my sentencing by the Judge who handled my case.

Just how many are affected by this "rather vulgar form of black-mail" is difficult to determine, but it should be remembered that miscarriage of justice cases – involving prisoners who have been wrongly convicted – were so common in our criminal justice system that this led to the setting up in 1997 of the Criminal Cases Review Commission (CCRC), which currently has a backlog of some 1000 cases and receives new cases at the rate of five per day (Wilson, 1999: 55). Similarly, a new pressure group – the United Campaign Against False Allegations of Abuse, which is an amalgam of other groups such as Falsely Accused Carers and Teachers (FACT) and Action Against False Allegations of Abuse (AAFAA) – has been set up to campaign and lobby for those who have been wrongly accused, sentenced and imprisoned in sexual abuse cases. Indeed, the first ever national conference of the United Campaign was held in London in September 2001, attended by some 200 delegates, and attracted a variety of speakers, including Neil and Christine Hamilton (see chapter 5).

The important points to grasp here are first and foremost that there will be some offenders who are wrongly convicted of sexual offences, but who will be required to work within a penal system that will expect those offenders to complete the SOTP. This is clearly unfair. Secondly, and perhaps our substantive point, the whole basis of the SOTP is that sexual offenders are "different" to other offenders, and indeed to us. They have "cognitive distortions", lack certain skills, and think and behave differently to you and me, and this is the "cause" of their offending. In short, cognitive behavioural therapy, on which the SOTP is grounded, is part of the positivistic paradigm that seeks to "uncover" what internal or, indeed, external factors create an offender. The difficulty here is, as we have explained in our opening chapter and reinforced with our discussion of paedophilia in chapter 2, that what we see as an "offence" can change over time, and between different cultures. What we call "crime", including sexual crimes, is not fixed for all time but responds to cultural norms and values, which can sometimes alter dramatically. Nor are these cultural norms and values necessarily agreed upon by all, and as a consequence "mixed messages" about what those values and norms are begin to confuse the picture, making it ever more difficult to determine what is "normal". This is an important point to remember, especially when set against the rather overblown claims made on behalf of some treatment programmes, and the increasingly diverse range of behaviours that have been subsumed under the label "paedophile".

The SOTP in HMP Wayland

HMP Wayland is a modern, purpose-built Category C training prison, opened in 1985, and set in the countryside of East Anglia between Thetford and Norwich. It can hold around 640 adult male prisoners, and in 1999–2000 cost some £9.5 million to run, of which £6.7 million was spent on staffing costs (*Welcome to Wayland Information Pack*). The prison has its own "Mission Statement" – a version of the prison service's own mission statement – which describes in simple language what it is that the prison hopes to achieve with the budget that is allocated. It states:

> We will maintain the confidence of the public, staff and prisoners by providing a secure but progressive regime giving opportunities for training, rehabilitation and individual self development to all those in our care.

> We are committed to an effective system of training and development for our staff and aim to set the standard of excellence for comparable prisons in HM Prison Service. (*Welcome to Wayland Information Pack*)

The prison was chosen as a place to observe the SOTP for three reasons. Firstly, the SOTP has been run at Wayland since the programme was introduced into the prison service in 1991. As such, staff working at the prison have built up considerable expertise in this area, and, as is clear from the prison's own mission statement, which emphasizes rehabilitation and a "progressive regime", this expertise is celebrated. Thus, we do not claim that the prison is necessarily "typical" of other prisons – even those that offer the SOTP. Secondly, we wanted to observe the SOTP in a penal environment that did not claim to operate as a "therapeutic community". This therefore facilitates an element of contrast with the more specialized regime at HMP Grendon. Finally, and a theme which we have been keen to emphasize throughout the book, key personnel working in the prison were female – most particularly the governor, Kate Cawley, and the principal officer in charge of the SOTP. (This principal officer did not want to be named, although she has accepted that it will be possible to identify her from descriptions in the book.) In this respect the prison is anything but "typical", for only 14 per cent of those in governor grades are female, and very few of these are actually in charge of a prison – especially a male prison (Bryans and Jones, 2001: 172).

The prison has four main residential units – A, B, C and D – with the latter three units each capable of holding 113 inmates, and A wing 138 prisoners. The SOTP takes place on E and F wings, which are located in their own grounds to the rear of A and B wings. E wing houses ninety-four inmates, and F wing forty prisoners who have achieved greater privileges under the incentives scheme, and who are regarded as a lower risk. On average fifteen inmates on E and F wings are life-sentenced prisoners. One governor, one principal officer, three senior officers, twenty-two officers, and two resident probation officers provide the staffing complement for the two wings, and, while there are basic education and gymnasium facilities available, the main activity is the SOTP. The daily routine that a prisoner on E or F wing would follow is outlined in table 4.2, although it should be noted that there is a separate programme for weekends.

Kate Cawley suggests that there are some particular difficulties about managing a prison that houses a large number of sex offenders. The first relates to integration. As she puts it, "generally speaking, they are not accepted by the rest of the prison population, and so you do end up having to operate separate regimes – keeping the sex offenders away from the rest of the prison population, and having them work in a separate place, and creating systems and

Table 4.2 Daily Routine (Monday), E and F wings,
HMP Wayland

Time	Activity
0810	Unlock – applications to see doctor to wing office
0810–0830	Breakfast by landing rotation
0815–0830	Daily medical treatment: F wing inmates collect full 24-hour treatment
0845	Inmates called to labour
0900	SOTP groups called – education as advertised
0900	Wing cleaners to work
1130	SOTP and labour return to wing
1130–1200	Outside exercise
1200	Lunch by landings: lock-up on completion
1350	Unlock
1350	Inmates to labour – education as advertised
1400	SOTP groups called
1625	SOTP and labour return to wing
1700	Tea by landing rotation and then lock-up

procedures which prevent the two from mixing." The reason for this is self-evident. As the female PO in charge of the SOTP explained, "if they mixed they would be severely beaten up." However, this should not be seen as applying in every case, and so, for example, there are twenty-two prisoners convicted of sex offences in the main prison population of Wayland. As Kate Cawley explains, this is "a curious thing . . . and in some circumstances it's because they have managed to keep their offence a secret". However, she also believes that some sex offenders are able to survive on "normal location" "because they are really quite strong characters who are able to dominate in that situation anyway. They are of sufficient strength in the sub-culture to simply ride over it and get away with it."

This raises the issue of prison cultures and hierarchies, for, despite the fact that prisons (and prisoners) can often seem similar, there are very lively cultures and sub-cultures in every jail. Most obviously there is the division between staff and inmates, but this simple division fails to acknowledge, for example, the various groupings of prisoners and indeed staff. In relation to the staff groupings, for example, there are male and female staff, uniformed and governor grades, specialist staff – such as physical education officers, dedicated search teams, works personnel and so forth – as well as a range of civilian staff who work in the prison every day. With regard to the prisoners, Kate Cawley describes the "prisoner hierarchy", which as far as she is concerned is too stereotypically seen as being simply based on offence – with "blaggers [prison slang for "armed robber"] at the top, and nonces [prison slang for "sex offender" – nonce being a derivative of "nonsense"] at the bottom".

> Actually at the top are strong characters, and as a generalization you might call them bullies. Some are strong characters, but they don't bully, but are simply opinion leaders on the wing. They may be figure-heads who are respected by the other prisoners, either because of the type of offence that they committed, or because of their stature, demeanour, or the fact that in some cases they are very intelligent. So, in those cases they get respect and position because they are able to help other prisoners with their complaints or litigation, or because they are seen as being able to sway staff or others in authority. If anyone has credibility with the other prisoners, they will be at the top of the tree. In the middle are a range of prisoners who don't quite have this credibility, and at the bottom it is usually sex offenders. However, it is not just sex offenders, but others who find it hard to assert themselves because they are young, or inexperienced in prison. And sometimes they are at the bottom just because they are not very strong characters, and are therefore just a prime target for other people to control.

The second issue that Kate Cawley feels has to be remembered when managing a prison with large numbers of sex offenders is one of staff manipulation. As she explains, "sex offenders are often very intelligent people, and they can come across as quite compliant, quite helpful, quite pro-authority, quite pro-establishment, but the flip-side of that is that sometimes they can be manipulative, and this can be dangerous . . . there can be an element of conditioning in their management, which sometimes makes things difficult." The female PO in charge of the SOTP provides some tangible examples of how sex offenders can be manipulative in relation to visiting arrangements, and how staff have to be careful about who visits – especially children. The only children who may visit someone on the SOTP – as long as they were not the victims of the offending – are their own children, children by adoption, and children of a partner that they have lived with prior to conviction.

So if, for example, "a new prisoner wanted his daughter to visit, we would write out to the parent or guardian and say 'Joe Bloggs wants his child to visit'. The parent or guardian would have to send back in photographs of the child, a copy of the birth certificate verified by the police, probation or social services, and we would then hold a copy at the gate to verify the child who arrives as being his." Thus the arrangements seem rigorous, but the PO explained that there were some who attempted to find ways of bypassing these arrangements, and that staff "were constantly being challenged about who can come in". Similarly, she explained that sex offenders were "constantly coming and giving information on each other" in an attempt to curry favour, or cause problems for someone else on the wing by suggesting that, for example, "so and so is only doing this to get parole." Some sex offenders might indeed only be completing the course in the hope of obtaining parole, but it was the staff's job to assess who was, or was not, committed to the programme.

The final issue was one of gender. Quite clearly it is unusual to have a woman in charge of a prison – especially a male prison with large numbers of sex offenders, and equally it was a woman who ran the prison's SOTP. How conscious were they of this when they went about their work? Kate Cawley felt that the fact that she was the governor allowed her to avoid dealing directly with issues of gender. "I'm more conscious of being the governor than being a woman. When I walk onto E and F wings I'm the governor, and that's my persona. The fact that I am also a woman and they are sex offenders is very secondary to the fact that I am also the governor." However, as might have been expected, it was rather different for the PO, not just because she was a lower rank, but also because she had to deal with the various realities, stresses and tensions associated with the SOTP. It was especially difficult, for example, when the offenders had to discuss issues related to their victims, for as often as not their victims were women. So, for example, some of the sex offenders:

> are intimidated because I am a woman, and some can be more verbal. They might be very shy and very withdrawn talking to me, but with a male staff member they will be more open and honest. On the other hand, it also works the other way around, and you can get the guy who's very aggressive and confrontational precisely because I am a woman. At the moment most are probably more shy of me because of my gender.

However, she wanted to work on the SOTP because it gave her "job satisfaction. It's knowing that you are preventing future victims. You tutor a group of eight, and if one doesn't reoffend you've saved so many victims." She went on to explain that the sex offenders were put under a "great deal of pressure" throughout the programme, and she described the essence of the programme as being:

> about behaviour, attitude, relationships, emotions, cognitions, his sexual interests and physical state. Everything that they say is taken note of, so as to enable him to see why he's offended. His account of his offence might just be "well, I was walking down the road, saw a woman and grabbed her and then raped her", and that might be the sum total of what he thinks about his offence. But when it comes to the active account block we take him through what he was thinking, what he was feeling prior to the rape, during the rape and what he was feeling after the rape. This is done over three days, with each individual in the "hot seat" for three sessions, over three separate days, talking about his offence.

She found it difficult to generalize which of the sessions would provide most of the sex offenders with some understanding of the damage that they had done – "every prisoner is different" – but she felt that most found the active account block "very difficult", as "they have a lot of barriers that they try to keep in place. Sometimes we have to remind them during this block why they are in the group, particularly when they have hit a difficult spot and they don't want to move on." Indeed, she thought of the programme as a "twenty-block jigsaw puzzle, and there's not one specific thing that you can say 'that's what helped', but it's the whole package". Nonetheless, she did feel that some of the offenders are transformed by the programme – "you do see differences, you do see a deeper understanding."

This faith in the SOTP was in marked contrast to her feelings about the recent publicity and tabloid interest in paedophiles. She stated quite simply that it "has been really unhelpful. It's about pointing a finger, all this 'naming and shaming'. You've had the *News of the World*, and people who've had their pictures put on lampposts, but you have got to give people an opportunity." She felt passionately that she was trying to prevent children from becoming the victims of sexual offences, but that "naming and shaming" was actually making the matter worse. She explained how this happened:

You could have the case of a guy who has been discharged, and he's been "named and shamed", and he's going to take the view that "well, they're going to get me anyway", and this gives him permission to reoffend. He thinks that he's going to go back to prison, and so that distortion allows him to offend again. You know, it's not about mums locking their daughters up. It's about society learning to let people exist within society, and that has to include sex offenders, even paedophiles . . . generally paedophiles will not go and grab a child off the street. They just don't work that way.

Kate Cawley is prepared to accept that people should be aware of who paedophiles are, and what they are doing, but that "naming and shaming" had left them with "a very particular set of challenges to overcome when they get out". Moreover, she did not feel that either the prison service or the probation service "had got their act together", in terms of how they are going to cope with sex offenders being released back into the community.

Evaluating the SOTP

As is obvious from some of her comments, the PO in charge of the SOTP at HMP Wayland had confidence in the ability of the programme to change sex offenders for the better. In this respect she is echoing a view about the ability of cognitive approaches generally to reduce an offender's level of reoffending. Thus, for example, we have already quoted James McGuire's conclusion that the net effect of treatment represented a reduction in recidivism of approximately ten percentage points. In some studies meeting certain additional criteria, the figures range from 20 to 30 per cent. And, in relation to sex offenders and paedophiles, McGuire (2000: 98–9) favourably comments on cognitive behavioural work with "very difficult kinds of behaviour" – including paedophilia, where "it has been possible to alter and ameliorate an individual's offence-proneness." As such, he cites two studies from the late 1970s and early 1980s. Similarly NACRO (1998: 6), referring to a Home Office evaluation of a sample of sex offenders on probation, found that the proportion of those participating in seven community-based treatment programmes who were reconvicted of a similar offence within two years "was around half the proportion of those under probation supervision without a treatment programme – 5 per cent as against 9 per cent".

Indeed, evaluation of this kind was built into the strategy that was announced by Kenneth Baker when he introduced the SOTP. For example, while acknowledging that "in the past [there has] been little systematic evaluation of sex offender treatment", from now on "the programmes introduced into the Prison Service will be evaluated for treatment integrity, their clinical impact and their impact on re-offending." However, it was also conceded that:

> The impact on offending is traditionally measured by recidivism rates, but for sex offenders the time between re-convictions can be lengthy and it may be many years before the effectiveness of the programmes can be judged. So, the aim is to develop shorter term objective measures of the clinical impact of the offender, which can be used in assessing the efficacy of the programmes and in deciding whether they continue to represent a worthwhile investment of resources. (Home Office, 1991: 11)

Nonetheless, there has been relatively little evaluation of the SOTP either in terms of its "clinical impact" or in relation to recidivism rates. Indeed, we have encountered only three evaluations in researching this book, although we accept that there may be others with which we are unfamiliar and which may have been published in more specialist academic journals. Perhaps we might conclude from this that the desire for evaluation has become less important, and that other – unacknowledged – criteria have been used to decide that the SOTP is a "worthwhile investment". Certainly the evidence from the most recent evaluation is at best mixed.

The most recent Home Office evaluation of the SOTP is by four forensic psychologists – Anthony Beech, Dawn Fisher, Richard Beckett and Ann Scott-Fordham (Beech et al., 1998). Their evaluation examined twelve treatment groups (about eight men in each group) in six different prisons. They looked at the effect of the SOTP on offenders' readiness to admit to offensive behaviour, pro-offending attitudes, social competence, and knowledge of relapse-avoidance techniques, with the aim of determining the programme's short-term effectiveness; to see whether treatment gains were maintained nine months after the end of treatment; and to determine whether treatment effectiveness was influenced by the type of offender. Their sample consisted of 100 men, but of note – and of special interest in relation to this chapter – this sample included eighty-two men who had sexually offended against children, and it was these eighty-two offenders who formed the basis of their evaluation. Thus their evaluation is specifically concerned with the impact of the SOTP on paedophiles. In relation to the short-term impact of the programme – which we might call its "clinical impact" – offenders were tested before and at the end of their treatment. The tests were designed to measure change in four areas:

- denial/admittance of deviant sexual interests and offending behaviours
- pro-offending attitudes
- predisposing personality factors
- relapse prevention skills.

As can be seen from these measures, the first relates to the "cognitive" aspect of the SOTP, which would involve the offender recognizing his patterns of "distorted" thinking, and understanding the impact which sexually abusive behaviour has on the victims of that behaviour. Relapse prevention skills – which in essence means getting the offender to recognize those situations that place him at risk of further offending, and generating effective strategies to deal with these – is more concerned with the "behavioural" aspect of the programme.

The evaluation broke the sample down into four groups, by distinguishing between their pre-treatment levels of pro-offending attitudes and social inadequacy (their level of "deviancy") and their level of admittance or denial (their level of "denial"). Thus the four groups were termed: low deviance/low denial; low deviance/high denial; high deviancy/low denial; and high deviancy/high denial. Further information about these groups is provided by the researchers:

> High deviancy men had nearly three times as many victims and were nearly twice as likely to have been convicted of a previous sexual offence as low deviancy men. They were also twice as likely to have committed offences against boys or both boys and girls, and twice as likely to have committed offences outside the family or a combination of outside and inside the family. *Men in low deviancy groups were nearly three times more likely to have committed offences against daughters and/or step-daughters within the family.* (Home Office, 1998b: 3; emphasis added)

Thus, the researchers make no attempt to see paedophilia as distinct from incest, despite (as we saw in chapter 2) the importance of acknowledging this definitional issue.

Overall, the short-term effectiveness of the programme was very positive, with significant improvements found in nearly all the denial/admittance measures in terms of less denial and more admittance. Similarly, relapse prevention scales, and all of the pro-offending attitudes measures, showed significant improvements, and, in particular, scales used to "measure distorted thoughts about children and the impact that abuse had on them showed striking improvements" (Home Office, 1998c: 2). However, the results in relation to longer-term changes are more varied. A follow-up study was conducted with fifty-six offenders who had finished the treatment programme, and who were asked to complete the original tests again. Of these fifty-six, thirty-two were still in prison, and twenty-four had been released. Overall, while the treatment changes brought about by the SOTP had been maintained, the comparison between those still in prison and those who had been released showed that the latter had "become significantly worse in their relapse prevention skills" (Home Office, 1998c: 2). Furthermore, by using the four groups that had been identified within the sample – from low deviance/low denial to high deviance/high denial – the researchers attempted to see whether there was a relationship between these groups and treatment change. In this case, "treatment change" was defined as change sufficient to reach a predefined minimum score on the range of tests that have been described, and the results are presented in table 4.3. In essence treatment was most successful for the low deviance/low denial group, which, as we have seen, were

Table 4.3 Treatment effects by pre-treatment deviancy and denial

Group	Number	Pro-offending attitudes	Pro-offending attitudes and predisposing personality	No change
Low deviancy/ low denial	32	27	19	5
Low deviancy/ high denial	24	17	4	7
High deviancy	21	9	3	12
Total	77	53	26	24

more than three times as likely to have committed offences within their family or step-family. Nearly two-thirds of this sample showed significant change on both pro-offending tests and predisposing personality traits, such as low self-esteem and under-assertiveness. However, the treatment was less successful for low deviancy/high denial groups, and was almost completely unsuccessful for the high deviancy group – which combined high and low denial groups. More than half of this latter group – some twelve offenders – showed no treatment change at all, and only three out of twenty-one showed change on both sets of tests. Overall it could be concluded from this evaluation that the SOTP was successful in increasing the levels of offenders' admittance of their offending behaviour, and that pro-offending attitudes, such as thoughts about having sexual contact with children, were reduced, as were levels of denial of the impact that sexual contact had had upon victims. However, it should be remembered that this treatment effect was confined largely to those offenders who had abused within their own family, and who were defined as "low deviance/low denial". Nor was a control group of similar offenders, who did not undergo the SOTP, used by the researchers to determine if the "treatment effect" comes from the programme itself or simply from other factors, such as remorse over time. After all, this group is seen as "low deviance/low denial". Of greater concern, there seems to have been little change as a result of the programme in those offenders who abused outside of the family – the "high deviance/high denial" group, with more than half showing no treatment change at all.

Conclusion

This chapter has been concerned with what happens to sex offenders and paedophiles after they have been imprisoned, and in particular we have looked closely at the SOTP. As such we have described how the SOTP was introduced into prisons in 1991, and how its roots come from cognitive behavioural therapy. And, in relation to this, we have described how cognitivism and behaviourism, when combined, are seen as being capable of sustaining change in offending behaviour. We have provided information about how the SOTP operates at HMP Wayland, and outlined the blocks that make up the core programme. Finally we have attempted to describe the most recent evaluation of the SOTP, the results of which we have characterized as being "mixed". In particular we have drawn attention to the fact that the SOTP seems to work best with those who have committed incest but is largely unsuccessful in dealing with those paedophiles who target children outside of their own families. This is no small matter, for the current obsession with paedophiles is particularly concerned with this latter group, and, if the prison service's major treatment programme does not work (although we accept that the evaluation was concerned with a small sample), then we must look in other directions for evidence as to how best to protect our children. Indeed this is the subject of our concluding chapter.

5

Protecting the Community

Is this guy a looker or a doer? Maybe he's both. The question is whether the police are under too much pressure to conduct all the investigations needed to find out.

Jim Reynolds, first head of Scotland Yard's Paedophilia Unit

It may surprise many to learn that the largest and best-resourced police force in the country, the Metropolitan Police, did not have a dedicated Paedophilia Unit before 1994. Until then, responsibility for identifying child sex offending rested with the Obscene Publications Squad, based at Charing Cross, which had been set up some thirty years earlier when Soho vice bosses were building empires from the burgeoning trade in pornography. By and large, this was adult, commercially produced material – in the parlance of the time, mucky films, mucky books, mucky magazines.

By the early 1990s, the computer-led revolution in production and delivery enabled the fantasies of paedophiles to be given much fuller expression. Now, so much child-centred material was being seized that Scotland Yard had to do some serious rethinking, and it decided to assign the investigation of all matters related to paedophiles to a new unit. The seismic shift in emphasis also extended to the terminology which the police used. "Child or kiddie porn" went out of fashion because it was felt to trivialize the nature of the crime. "Child abuse images" gave a truer picture. Equally significant was the placing of the unit in the International and Organized Crime Branch, along with the Flying Squad and the War Crimes Unit. Symbolically, at least, the paedophile was no longer just the sad loner in the raincoat masturbating in a West End cinema but one link in a global chain of profit-making derived from the rape and exploitation of children.

But symbolism often obscures understanding, and this chapter seeks to explore the complexities of paedophile abuse as seen through the prism of law enforcement. Given that we don't know whether child sex crime has increased in recent years, why are there so many more police investigations? Has the pressure to investigate – especially in "historical" cases of abuse – led to miscarriages of justice? How common is the organized paedophile "ring"? And, above all, what part has the Internet played in the pattern of behaviour of offenders? Because some of those we have interviewed are serving law enforcement officers, we have respected their wish to remain anonymous where necessary.

Cyber policing

In 1995, the Obscene Publications Unit of Greater Manchester Police seized about a dozen images of child pornography during the whole year. They were all in video or stills format and, according to the head of the unit, Detective Inspector Terry Jones – one of the country's foremost investigators of child sex abuse – they were "grainy, poor quality material, like watching child abuse through a snow-storm". In 1999, his team recovered 41,000 images, all, bar three, in computer format. "Now", he says, referring to late 2001, "we've stopped counting, the amount is so enormous." One man recently targeted by his unit possessed a collection of 50,000 images plus more than three gigabytes of movie files. The reasons for this flood of material are twofold. One is technology. Video films used to require specialist equipment and a level of expertise to produce. The availability of digital cameras has both simplified the process and transformed the reproduction of images. The other is the avail-ability of the Internet. Terry Jones: "In the mid-1990s, our biggest ever haul of pornographic videos was 1200 in a single year. That may sound a lot, but compare it to the sheer volume of information which can be stored on computer. One floppy disk equals about 700 pages of text. One CD-Rom can carry the equivalent of 650 full-length novels. In another five years, who knows how much stuff will be circulating?"

The fact that the Internet seems to have taken over our lives in so many (largely legitimate and beneficial) ways should not blind us to the speed with which this has happened. We should remember, too, that the world of law enforcement is still grappling with this new phenomenon. After all, the first conviction (of a computer consultant) for receiving child pornography via the Internet was as recent as 1996. And the first operation to target paedophiles using the Internet for communicating with one another, Operation Starburst, took place in 1998. This case, in which information from the US Customs Service led to the identification of a researcher at Birmingham University who had stored some 1800 paedophile images on the university computer, was handled by the Commercial Vice Unit of the West Midlands Police. But the international ramifications of the Internet made it inevitable that, henceforth, the national agencies NCIS (National Criminal Intelligence Service), NCS (National Crime Squad) and HM Customs, with their resources and expertise, would play a larger and larger role.

However, even the NCS was staggered by the scale of the enterprise it uncovered in what became the most notorious Internet paedophile investigation of the 1990s, Operation Cathedral. The so-called Wonderland Club (presumably named after Lewis Carroll's creation) was a network which operated for four years in thirteen countries as a kind of global swapshop in child pornography. Like any club, it had a chairman, a treasurer and a board of members. It had a set of rules, called the Traders Security Handbook. Unlike any legitimate club, the entry requirement was outlandish – 10,000 fresh pornographic images of children. When the police eventually broke up the network, they seized a staggering 750,000 individual images and 1800 digitized video clips of prepubescent children – some of them only a few months old.

Inevitably, operations like Cathedral raise questions, such as what proportion of users of child pornography abuse children as well. It is a difficult question to answer and one that divides the experts. Research conducted by the FBI in 1998 suggested that under half of collectors of material had, as far as investigators could tell, committed offences of abuse. On the other hand, an unpublished study by US Customs estimated that only about 20 per cent had not been abusers as well. The former chief constable of Gloucestershire, Tony Butler, told us that, "for every 100 people you arrest for possession of child pornography, fewer than ten are abusers." With that kind of disparity of assessment, perhaps we are just as well served with an old police maxim: "Not all lookers are doers. But you never arrest a doer without finding child pornography as well."

But what role is played by the pornography? British law enforcement has been much influenced by studies carried out at the Department of Applied Psychology at the University of Cork into the impact of viewing on offending behaviour – the COPINE Project. The conclusion is that there is no neat, simple link between the two, but some of the on-line "consumers" say revealing things during their interviews. Here is a sample:

> [Viewing pornography on the Internet] made me want to do the things I wanted to do. It gave me more courage to do them . . . knowing that I've seen it on there . . . they were doing it . . . I can do it.

> I was finding more explicit stuff on the computer and I was looking at the computer and thinking, oh . . . they're doing it . . . it can't be that bad.

> I would say it fuelled my interest that I had anyway, that was in me . . . but it seemed to reinforce it and . . . made me want to act on it.

> It wasn't on the first night that I abused, but probably looking at the images on the Internet then . . . I seemed to notice her more.

If those comments are representative, it seems that, for many, the Internet validates a form of behaviour which they know to be, at best, deviant and, at worst, unlawful. But given that we know how manipulative and secretive paedophiles can be, there is another layer of truth that needs to be uncovered. Has the Internet brought to the attention of the police (and researchers) abusive activity which has been going on for many years but for which the perpetrator has never been caught? DI Terry Jones, from the Greater Manchester Police, is too experienced to make glib judgments:

> What we do know is that around 70 per cent of Internet paedophiles have no previous convictions. One interpretation is that many of them *have* been abusing but, for a variety of possible reasons, have never come to our notice. After all, many of these images we are now seeing used to be part of private collections. Now they are being traded on the Internet – and some of them (we don't know how

many) are a record of actual abuse by the collector. We know about Fred West and Ian Brady, who taped or filmed their abuse, but how many others are out there?

However, some of those who have no previous [convictions] probably have not offended before, so it is clear that something has inhibited them from offending earlier in life. It might have been the feeling of being isolated, of being on their own. After all, at one time, if you wanted to meet and connect with other paedophiles, it would have taken some effort. You would probably have had to join a semi-clandestine organization like the Paedophile Information Exchange. Now, that contact can be made at the click of a mouse. And you know there are lots of people like you out there.

But there is yet another interpretation which could be placed on that figure of 70 per cent of Internet paedophiles with no previous criminal history. Perhaps the Internet has merely given a new space to "fantasy users" who have no intention of physically abusing a child but who get their thrills from acting out adult–child sex through chat rooms. This proposition has been put forward by Kimberley S. Young, founder of the Centre for Online Addiction, when she spoke at the annual convention of the American Psychological Association in August 2000. She says:

> The idea of becoming someone different lures many users into excessive Internet use because of the fantasy escape that the activity provides. . . . It is important to emphasize that what a participant says and does on-line does not necessarily represent what he or she desires in real life. A woman who role-plays a rape or bondage fantasy does not desire to be raped or tortured in real life. . . . Clinical research suggests that deviant sexual discussions that take place on-line do not always come from individuals with any pre-existing disposition to deviancy.

As we suggested at the outset of this chapter, the Internet is such a new means of communication that it is far too soon for fully formed theories about its impact on crime. And it could be argued that, whatever else consumers of child abuse images are guilty of, they are aiding and abetting those who produce the material which fuels their fantasies. The COPINE researchers put it like this: "At its worst, photographs of child sexual abuse are photographs of a crime in progress." That is graphically borne out by the images found in the possession of the eight men arrested in the UK during Operation

Cathedral. They represented the torture and degradation of thousands of children all over the world – children manacled to beds with collars around their necks, children blindfolded and suspended by their wrists from an overhead rail, babies in nappies and so on. This abuse is being perpetrated only because there is a market for it, and the market is growing year on year.

A senior customs source remarked: "this is commercially produced and distributed material, and it is much more prevalent than it was five or six years ago. To give you an example of the profits being made, a married couple in the US, the Reedys, were making $1,500,000 a month selling access to child abuse sites on the Internet. And of course, where so much money is at stake, organized crime is taking over. This is an interesting development because, a few years ago, non-paedophiles didn't want to get involved with a 'dirty' trade. They took the view: 'they're all scum.' But money is persuasive, and now they're churning the stuff out, particularly in places where gangsterism is rife, like Russia." The result is that Russia is now the source of some of the most hard-core child abuse imagery circulating on the Internet. In March 2001, a joint operation between the US and Russian police broke up a gang running a website called "Blue Orchid" from an apartment in Moscow. The site featured the sexual abuse of young Russian boys, and when the police raided the flat they found a number of the boys lined up in front of the video cameras.

There are some who see the debate about this material as equivalent to the argument about drugs and that, while the producers and dealers should be deterred, the users deserve compassion rather than punishment. We believe that this is a false comparison and that those who get their sexual gratification in this way are the cause, whether knowing or unknowing, of appalling child abuse. The question of whether any distinction should be made in sentencing terms between producers and users has rightly exercised the Sentencing Advisory Panel. Responding to a request for advice from the Court of Appeal, it issued a consultation paper in January 2002, inviting views on a sentencing regime for those who make, distribute or possess indecent images of children. It is a sign of the rapid increase in the number of cases of Internet abuse which are being investigated and prosecuted that this consultation paper was issued only a year after the sentence for possession of such material was raised to a maximum of five years and for production and distribution to ten years.

While the deterrence effect of longer sentences is arguable, it is right that the courts should be able to punish the worst offenders appropriately. What does concern us, though, is a change in the law to tackle on-line "grooming" by paedophiles, making it both a criminal and a civil offence to meet or approach a child with a sexual intent. This began with a commitment by the then home secretary, Jack Straw, in May 2001. The timing was hardly accidental, coming as it did a month before the general election and in response to a manifesto pledge by the Conservatives. Like much legislation hatched in haste, it looks as thin as gossamer when subjected to scrutiny. Remember, we are talking about a successful application for a paedophile prevention order *before* an offence has actually taken place. Apart from the protection afforded by the Human Rights Act (a difficulty acknowledged by the former Home Office minister Beverley Hughes in July 2001), the idea has few advocates in the police, who will have to enforce it. After all, if forces needed to be cajoled and prodded into applying for anti-social behaviour orders – because of the cost, time, paperwork, and dubious value involved in persuading courts to impose them – even where there was clear evidence of the crime and vandalism committed, what is the prospect of their being eager to embrace the new paedophile orders? In keeping with a number of much-trumpeted ideas to emanate from the New Labour Home Office since 1997, it has plenty of sound but precious little bite.

A far more pragmatic way forward is that proposed in a report entitled *Chat Wise, Street Wise – Children and Internet Chat Services* by the Internet Crime Forum, published in May 2001. The forum includes representatives of the Association of Chief Police Officers, child welfare groups, Internet companies and the Home Office. It proposed that the chat rooms and bulletin boards should be monitored by specialist cyber "police" for inappropriate or sexually explicit language or attempts by adults (where they can be detected) to make contact with children. Sites which are deemed "paedophile-free" would have a special kitemark or badge of excellence. The forum also recommended that a new police helpline should be established to give advice to parents or children whose suspicions are aroused by any of the people using chat rooms. No one is pretending that this is a failsafe answer, but it seems to us more sensible than a legislative change which raises expectations yet is little enforced.

Undoubtedly, the Internet has presented law enforcement with a major and unprecedented challenge. A senior source at the National Criminal Intelligence Service says that the Internet is responsible for a big increase in the number of child pornography cases investigated by the police. And the NCIS, in a report entitled *Project Trawler: Crime on the Information Highways*, points out how the new medium has transformed the international trade in abusive material from one based largely on the import of magazines and videos – which could be intercepted as they entered the country – to an electronic transaction in which images can be scanned in and stored as computer files. It concludes: "With the Internet, there is no border control and (often) no tangible goods, complicating law enforcement's task of detecting the crime and obtaining the evidence."

We would argue that this is an unduly bleak assessment and contributes to the aura of pessimism about the Internet which, for the sake of clear-headedness, needs to be dispelled. After all, downloading imagery onto a disk or saving it on the hard drive constitutes unlawful possession in exactly the same way as being caught with a shelf full of hard-core videos. In such a case, the evidence is indisputable whatever the *mens rea* of the user. Compare that with the difficulty of proving, in law, that a man hanging around the gates of a primary school had an evil intent. In other, more technical ways, too, which the police are reticent about discussing, someone using a computer – even when they have not saved anything – will frequently leave a "trace" which may be used against them in court. And new software has given a powerful fillip to police investigations into the use of Internet chat rooms to peddle abusive images of children. This was seen to good effect in April 2002 in Operation Magenta, in which twenty-seven people were arrested in the UK's largest Internet paedophile operation.

One of the most notable features of this inquiry – in which thirty-four forces, led jointly by Greater Manchester and Hertfordshire, participated – was the close involvement of an Internet filter company, SurfControl. The piece of kit it developed cut dramatically the amount of time needed to filter out innocent chat room "traffic" taking place all over the world and home in on illicit transactions in the UK, providing both names and addresses. Thus thirty hours of monitoring by detectives identified seventy-five suspects. To perform the same task manually would have taken the team 300 hours. This is not merely a matter of speed or boosting the statistics. As DI Terry Jones points out, it has contributed to a sea-change in the way paedophile activity is addressed. "We have never had the opportunity to be proactive before. In the past, we have been able to deal with paedophile crime only when the victim has disclosed the offence – and, as we know, this can be twenty or thirty years later. Now, with this technology, we can take the fight to the abuser – and perhaps stifle the offending before it develops."

One issue which should not be downplayed is the preservation of the electronic evidence needed to secure a conviction. In the words of a senior police trainer, "we in the UK are coming from way behind the starting-line" in this respect, compared, for example, to those in American law enforcement. It is also true that technological devices, such as encryption – where some kind of code or key is needed to access the material – and stegnography – where the pornographic image is hidden behind something innocuous – provide extra layers of security. And some paedophiles have far more advanced skills than either the majority of police officers investigating them or other practitioners, such as probation officers and social workers, assigned to supervise those who are convicted. But the idea that the Internet is some kind of devil's playground for the computer generation overstates the case. As our Customs source says:

> Sure, some paedophiles are good with computers, but we tend to overrate their high-tech skills. There's also a false impression of the number of organized networks. The press loves to use the phrase "paedophile ring", when all that has happened is that one person has sent another some banned material. Most paedophiles are not in organized groups. And those that are (like the Wonderland Club) don't fit the pattern of organized crime, which has a hierarchical structure. Here, the links tend to be lateral and much looser.

Entrapment

The Internet does have one undeniable advantage for the paedophile – anonymity. For someone who is chronically insecure and asocial, it is plainly easier to wander into a cyber chat room protected by a bogus name than it is to wander into a park and hover near a playground talent-spotting. It is also easier and safer to download hard-core pornography from the net than to go to an adult-only video store or dealer and buy it (though some Internet paedophiles also have large video collections). However, anonymity is a two-way street. It can work for the law enforcers just as effectively as for the abusers, and in the United States it has been a powerful weapon in the hands of a special FBI squad, whose agents pose as children in order to entrap paedophiles. The team was set up in 1995, and more than 400 of the 500 people arrested in this way have been convicted.

One of those caught by such a "sting" operation was David Steinheimer, an American mature student (aged thirty-eight) doing a PhD at the University of Aberdeen. In October 2000, he travelled from Aberdeen to Houston, Texas, to meet an Internet contact whom he believed to be a thirteen-year-old boy. Steinheimer had answered an advert for a pen-friend and had sent the "boy" sexual images, including four pictures of children involved in sex acts. When he arrived in Houston, Steinheimer was arrested and charged with six separate offences. The court sentenced him to seven years and three months in jail.

But this is possible in the United States only because its federal law, heavily influenced by the need to use unorthodox tactics against organized crime, permits entrapment. In the UK, such sting operations, using undercover police officers as *agents provocateurs*, have invariably come to grief and would not be sanctioned by the Crown Prosecution Service. However, in many police forces, officers tackling paedophile crime go on-line to monitor activity and, where they are aware that a meeting with a child is being arranged, will mount an operation to make an arrest. Indeed, Thames Valley Police carried out such an operation in 2000. And given the vogue for more proactive law enforcement, coupled with the amount of media coverage of Internet child abuse, it would be unwise to rule out a policy change which would bring the UK closer to the American model.

As a final point on the Internet, it is worth recording that the age of those accessing and distributing child pornography appears to be coming down. Police officers consistently report that teenagers are not only the unwilling dupes of cyber paedophiles but, frequently, the instigators of illicit activity, too. National Crime Squad officers involved in 2001 in a multi-country Internet operation, codenamed Landmark, found disturbing evidence of teenage boys and girls videoing themselves masturbating and then posting the images on newsgroup websites. Given that, generally, young people are far more computer-literate than their parents' generation, it should hardly come as a surprise that some turn their technical knowledge to deviancy, but it challenges our often stereotyped notions of the adult abuser in his thirties, forties or fifties, seeking virgin prey. As DI Terry Jones says:

What alarms me is the prospect for current and future offending patterns of adolescents accessing this material. To put it bluntly, the ones who are masturbating to material now can be expected to put their fantasies into practice sometime in the future if they have the opportunity. Given that the research shows that a third of all sex crime against children may be committed by adolescents, this is very frightening.

In March 2001, Terry Jones's team led a nationwide operation against Internet child abusers, targeting forty-eight suspects – the aptly named Operation Appal. Six were under seventeen and one was a thirteen-year-old. When arrested, he had hidden in his bedroom, 321 child abuse images downloaded from the Internet, including those depicting the abuse of babies. There was much talk in the newspapers when he became the youngest person in Britain to be placed on the Sex Offender Register, but, sadly, it is a harbinger of things to come.

Child protection

The speed with which computers and the Internet have transformed our society and many aspects of high-tech crime is unprecedented. It has also had consequences for the police which can't be ignored. In recent years, chief constables have tended to take their lead from government and set their priorities accordingly. In the mid-1990s, as the recorded crime figures soared apparently out of control, they were urged to target car crime and burglary. Towards the end of the decade, after a number of reports showing the link between alcohol and violence, this, too, became a focus. But though protecting the community from paedophiles has been moving up the government's agenda since 1997, the police have been left confused about where they should be directing their resources, as the former chief constable of Gloucestershire, Tony Butler, explains:

> It is well known that the police are set performance targets by government, and usually this happens after informed debate. Take the Macpherson Report [into the murder of Stephen Lawrence]. The police may not have agreed with all the conclusions, but there was no doubt in anyone's mind that tackling racist attacks was henceforth a key priority. But there has been no such national debate

about child sex offenders. All we've had is the *News of the World* campaign and the fire-fighting which the police have been forced to do against vigilantes. The whole issue has been tackled on a piece-meal basis.

So what are the practical consequences of this lack of clarity?

No one in politics is talking about the cost of managing the Internet. As chief constable, I had to decide where to direct my manpower and resources. Should I be spending more money putting dozens of officers in front of computer terminals intervening in chat rooms? Or should I be boosting the Child Protection Unit to deal with routine abuse cases and liaising with the other agencies in the field on a public education programme to encourage children to come forward early and report abuse rather than suffer for years in silence? It's a choice, and the *News of the World* doesn't have to make that choice.

Are you telling me that the traditional pattern of child abuse has been completely changed by the Internet? And even if it has, what is the best tactic to disrupt what is happening? Before throwing millions at something sexy like the High Tech Crime Unit [shared between the National Criminal Intelligence Service and National Crime Squad], should we not be seeking to build on community-based multi-agency child protection programmes which have been in place for ten years? The National Crime Squad is getting extra cash to patrol the Internet, but it has no child protection experience whatsoever. The fact is that most of the real work is being done by the police forces themselves.

The issue of resources is, of course, always close to the heart of senior police officers, and it will be no surprise to learn that, for Jim Reynolds, who headed Scotland Yard's Paedophilia Unit for more than four years until 1998, it is a central aspect of the child protection debate which the country should have had some years back:

When I retired, the unit had fifteen detectives in it. Three years later, it still has fifteen, despite the huge increase in workload. At the level I was working, no one would say that targeting paedophiles was unimportant, but I was competing with units like the Flying Squad. So, if I said at a Yard strategy meeting that we were planning some raids the week after next, and, at the same time, the Super in the Flying Squad said they had intelligence that a gang was about to pull off a diamond heist at the Millennium Dome, where do you think the resources would go?

Similarly, there is a great deal of talk about the Sex Offender Register, and in each police force there is someone responsible for maintaining and updating it. But, frankly, most forces don't have the funds to do the job properly. So, we sit around a table with social services, probation and other professionals and we decide whether an individual is low, medium, high or very high risk. But then what do we do? We just don't have the staffing to monitor them – and neither do probation.

Greater Manchester Police's Obscene Publications Unit had six officers when it was formed in 1978, and it still has six (though it has been renamed the Abusive Images Unit). And DI Terry Jones sees no conflict between his work and that of the area child protection teams:

I think it's a mistake to see Internet abuse as somehow separate from the great bulk of abuse which goes on. Because of the Internet, we have an unprecedented opportunity to identify those people with an apparent sexual interest in children who we may not have known about before. Arresting them is a form of intervention in their offending cycle – hopefully an early enough one. And if they end up on the Sex Offender Register, at least their names are known to the police and probation and social services. In some cases, of course, an Internet operation leads you to someone guilty of serious sexual abuse over many years. In Operation Appal, for example, one of those arrested was Patrick John Rendall, a scoutmaster who pleaded guilty to twenty-two offences, including rape and abuse of a twelve-year-old child. He'd been abusing this boy for more than three years and asked for 281 other offences to be taken into consideration! Who would say that that operation wasn't worthwhile?

Having considered this carefully and spoken to most of the key law enforcement players, we have come to the view that there is clearly some kind of continuum between abuse via the Internet and abuse *per se*. Terry Jones has given one example of how an Internet operation led to the arrest of a serious abuser. But the link works both ways. He could also have mentioned the case of Gary Salt, whose arrest in Stockport in 1998 by officers from a Greater Manchester Police Child Protection Unit, following a "routine" complaint from a family member, was the catalyst for the worldwide Internet investigation Operation Cathedral. When the police raided Salt's home, they found 42,000 child sex images on his computer, and it was those images which helped uncover the activities of the Wonderland Club.

Rediscovering the past

Whatever proportion of child sex contacts are made via the Internet, the bulk of police work is rightly concentrated on those settings in which paedophile abuse most often takes place – families, schools, sports clubs, church and scout groups, and the myriad everyday contacts which enable the ill-intentioned to exploit the vulnerable (as Terry Jones points out, the babysitter is the most common source of extra-familial abuse). But some police inquiries have been highly controversial – those into allegations of abuse at residential care homes and schools, often going back several decades. In the light of Tony Butler's observation that policing child abuse has developed piecemeal, it is a phenomenon which raises an interesting question: are the police responding to heightened public concern, or is that concern being stimulated partly by awareness of more police activity? Frustratingly, this is yet another question which is easier to pose than to answer, but all of the law enforcement officers to whom we have spoken acknowledge that they have been under greater pressure to investigate such cases over the past decade than ever before.

A number of things explain this. This is a period when society has grown steadily less tolerant of a range of activities once treated by the police as low priority – drink-driving, domestic violence and date-rape, to name a few. In the area of sex crime, the woeful conviction figures for rape have led to high-profile campaigns by womens' groups and much self-examination by criminal justice agencies such as the Crown Prosecution Service. Given that there are so many more organizations working in the field of children's rights and protection, it was inevitable that child sexual abuse would demand a higher priority. And with the law being asked to address other past wrongs, some going back half a century or more – such as the War Crimes Act of 1991 – claims of abuse, whether current or past, could no longer be filed under the dismissive acronym NFA ("no further action", in police jargon).

In our introduction, we made it clear that we did not intend to disinter any of these so-called historical child abuse cases and subject them to forensic scrutiny. As we pointed out, Richard Webster has already done that in his slim – but important – work *The Great Children's Home Panic*, and the respected investigative journalist Bob Woffinden has also drawn attention to disturbing features of some of the convictions.

But it is pertinent to raise the issue here for two reasons. Firstly, the fact that some of these cases got off the ground at all bears directly on our central premise that, as a society, we have become obsessed with paedophilia. After all, what other field of crime has led to the investigation of hundreds of serious allegations going back decades, not following a change in the law (as was the case with war crimes) but because the police themselves decided to mount such inquiries? Secondly, we believe that some of the tactics used by the police to secure evidence would be generally regarded as unacceptable if the alleged crime was not child sex abuse. At one time, this argument was on the margins of respectability, but it has moved into the mainstream with the setting up of an all-party parliamentary group to investigate miscarriages (in October 2001). And when you have the Lord Chief Justice expressing grave concern that some of the convictions in care-home prosecutions may be unsafe, it is surely time to take notice (*The Independent*, 23 November 2001).

Pointing out that the issue had already been raised by the Criminal Cases Review Commission (a third of all new cases considered by the CCRC involve sex offenders), Lord Woolf said that the recollections of former residents of children's homes who made allegations about "very old offences" may not be accurate, and he warned that plans to relax the rules of evidence so that juries could be made aware of a defendant's previous convictions might increase the risk of injustice. One of the principal issues here is the practice, in many police forces, of tempting potential witnesses to come forward by dangling before them the prospect of compensation from the Criminal Injuries Compensation Board. We examine this so-called trawling in more detail in a moment, but at this stage it is worth recording the response of the police to these concerns. Jim Reynolds is somewhat surprised at the fuss:

> If people who genuinely have been assaulted get a few bob as a result of a successful prosecution, what's wrong with that? Like it or not, we live in a compensation culture now. Of course, I'm not advocating that people invent allegations just to make money – nor do I doubt that these things can and do happen. The police just have to be more careful – and the lawyers as well. But what isn't always appreciated is that the police don't have a choice. They're obliged to investigate when serious allegations are made, whether they relate to events which happened twenty-five years ago or yesterday. Look at it from the point of view of the victim. Should you be treated any less

seriously because the abuse happened all those years ago and you felt unable to come forward before?

Of course not. But if you look at it from the point of view of the accused, you see a rather different conundrum. Those children who say they were abused many years ago are now adults, and they know the value of money. Furthermore, quite frequently, they are adults who have been in prison or whose motives for coming forward may not be entirely scrupulous. In a Lords debate in October 2001, Lord Lucas put it like this: "I do not like the practice of trawling. It is too much of a temptation, particularly where people being asked are themselves criminals or damaged people for one reason or another. It invites false accusation, especially when there is no penalty for making a false accusation." (There is, of course, the sanction of a perjury charge for giving false evidence in court, but we are not aware of any witness in a child sex abuse case being prosecuted for perjury.)

In the 1970s, Terry Hoskin was headmaster of a residential institution in Widnes, Cheshire (a type of establishment known as a community home with education). He served as national president of the Association of Community Homes and was invited to Buckingham Palace in recognition of his achievements. But in 1996, after a two-year police investigation, he was charged with twenty-one counts of physical and sexual abuse of the children formerly in his care. A number of those making the allegations either were, or had been, in prison. Many of the details in the complaints were glaringly inconsistent. But he was sentenced to eight years in jail – of which he served just over four. Many people who have studied his case are convinced that he is the victim of a gross miscarriage, and, when we met him at the home of a social worker also fighting a conviction for child sex abuse, we wanted to know why a jury had been prepared to believe the evidence of convicted criminals rather than that of a respected head teacher? Terry Hoskin:

It can be explained by one word. Volume. In other words, the police had collected statements from enough people alleging abuse that the jury must have thought, "well, there's no smoke without fire – they can't all be making it up." The quality of the evidence didn't appear to matter. Nor that some of the details appeared to have been supplied by the police during interviews. I can't prove that the police used the prospect of money as an inducement, but in one case which

I know of, a tariff of compensation was handed out to potential witnesses. It was an actual list, and it said "buggery – x amount; indecent assault – x amount; physical harm – x amount". You could say it was a shopping list of what you could get for a conviction.

And because of the heightened concern about paedophilia, are the police under more pressure now to carry out such investigations than they were ten or fifteen years ago? "Well, there must be pressure from somewhere, because the finance for all these inquiries appears to be no object. There are so many investigations going on that I dread to think of the cost. The police are travelling out of county. They are clocking up huge amounts of overtime. They are even going abroad to interview witnesses. I would really like to know how much it is costing the taxpayer to convict innocent people."

Unfortunately, that kind of information does not appear to be held centrally, but we have collated data which gives some idea of the sheer scale of institutional child abuse inquiries. In the summer of 2001, thirty-six of the forty-three police forces in England and Wales were carrying out at least one such investigation. Thirty-one of them responded to a circular from the Association of Chief Police Officers, asking how many abuse inquiries they had carried out since 1993. The figure was 124, with the number of alleged victims totalling 5477. Bearing in mind that some of the forces may have included information relating to major inquiries only, it doesn't require a leap of the imagination to infer that an extraordinary amount of police time and expenditure was being allocated to child sex abuse allegations. Given that there is very little hard evidence to show that the amount of abuse has increased dramatically in the same period, one must conclude that social/political concern about paedophile behaviour is the spur to such activity.

There is one feature of such investigations which marks them out from almost all other police work. It may be stating the obvious but, as a rule, the trigger for an inquiry is a crime. The police then set out to find out who committed it by amassing evidence. The reverse is true of retrospective child abuse inquiries. Here, the starting-point is the name of a suspect, and detectives have to establish that he or she has committed a crime, sometimes a decade or two earlier. This is generally achieved by what the police call "corroboration by quantity" – in other words, finding enough witnesses whose allegations are credible. Inevitably, this means seeking out complainants and

persuading them to talk. The only other recent field of police investigation in the UK which bears comparison is war crimes. But it is
significant that, in the period of active inquiries by the war crimes
units in England and Scotland, 1991–2000, only two prosecutions
were brought out of 400 suspects investigated. It is true, of course,
that the crimes under scrutiny were committed fifty or sixty years
ago rather than ten or twenty, but many cases foundered, not because of paucity of evidence, but because of a lack of enthusiasm
within both senior levels of the police and the legal establishment,
perhaps reflecting the public view that this was a matter better left
to historical research rather than the law (Silverman, 2000). There
was no such failure of nerve in child sex abuse inquiries.

Though we have raised a number of questions about the methods
used to obtain convictions in such cases, we do not suggest that the
majority of those who make allegations of abuse do so for money,
nor do we underestimate the difficulty facing the police. Many paedophiles are middle class, articulate and in positions of trust and
responsibility, giving them a protective shield that may be hard to
penetrate. Moreover, they know that their victims will invariably
find it difficult to break cover by making an accusation. It is these
advantages which have often enabled the abuser to escape detection
for years.

In 1997, Scotland Yard's Paedophilia Unit coordinated what, at
that time, was the largest series of raids against a paedophile network in the UK. Called Operation Clarence, the targets were mainly
music teachers employed at a number of prestigious fee-paying
schools. For Jim Reynolds, the case was symptomatic of a general
problem.

> It never ceased to amaze me that we would make an arrest of some-
> one, such as a music teacher, and we would discover that he had a
> history of abusing but no one had ever checked his antecedents. We
> would contact his previous head and ask why the suspect had left the
> school and he would say: "Well, between you and me there was some
> inappropriate behaviour with a pupil, but it didn't go down on his
> records." These sort of schools are the most reluctant to talk about
> child sex abuse because of the scandal and the fear of putting off
> parents. What often happens is that they take the easy way out. They
> confront the abuser, he says he's never been so insulted in his life,
> it's all lies etc., hands in his resignation and he's off. Well, what a
> wonderful solution for all concerned. The school avoids a fuss. The
> parents and the child concerned avoid a traumatic court case – and,

of course, even though the abuse took place, there may not even be enough evidence to bring a prosecution.

But what happens? The music teacher is well qualified, he sees a job advert elsewhere, the head there is desperate to fill the position before the beginning of the next term, so he's hired and the cycle of abuse continues. Why doesn't someone just pick up the phone and ask questions?

This kind of collusive secrecy – which applies just as much to other professions, such as the clergy or doctors – can make the investigation of paedophilia as difficult as the investigation of organized crime. The buzzwords in modern policing may be "intelligence-led" and "proactive" but, as Terry Jones says: "Forget the media obsession with stranger danger. The overwhelming majority of offenders know their victim, either through family ties or another relationship, and 80 per cent of the abuse takes place in the home of the victim or the home of the offender. Look how the 'serial boyfriend' worms his way into the affections of a succession of women so that he can achieve his real purpose, which is to get close to their pre-teenage daughters, or sons. How on earth do you proactively police that scenario?"

Mapping the future

One of the most commendable features of government law and order policy since 1997 has been the emphasis on multi-agency working. New Labour used its long years in opposition to good advantage, rethinking a crime strategy based predominantly on the police and probation and recognizing that social services, housing, health and education all had a role to play. The Crime and Disorder Act 1998 – which, among a raft of measures, introduced community protection orders to restrict the movement of released paedophiles – was the first legislative fruit of this thinking. Another significant development was Whitehall support for an initiative which had begun as a pilot in 1995 in two areas of Greater Manchester – Bury and Rochdale – and which can now be seen as having immense potential for finding a better way of managing the risk posed to the community by paedophiles.

This initiative was the so-called Multi-Agency Risk Panels, and they brought together the police, probation service and other local agencies to share information about high-risk offenders living in the area. Having worked successfully in Bury and Rochdale, the scheme was extended to all ten districts in Greater Manchester in the autumn of 1997. Thereafter, panels were introduced across England and Wales but, despite an acknowledgement by the then home secretary, Jack Straw, that they were an important contribution to public safety, their implementation was patchy and standards varied greatly. It was not until the Criminal Justice and Court Services Act 2000 that a statutory duty was placed on chief officers of police and probation to initiate multi-agency arrangements to manage the risk posed by sexual and violent offenders and to spread best practice.

The risk panels have been renamed Multi-Agency Public Protection Panels (MAPPPs), and at the time of writing (before the first annual report on their functioning has been completed, let alone published) it is too soon to judge their contribution to community safety. It is significant, however, that the reverberations from Sarah Payne's murder have touched this development too, because in December 2001, the home secretary, David Blunkett, made a commitment that, alongside the professionals sitting on the MAPPPs, he would make provisions for bringing in parents from the local community. We would comment that this is a far easier promise to make than to implement. A well-placed official in the National Probation Service, with a police background, put it like this: "Following the *News of the World*'s campaign for a Sarah's Law, we have all got the message that there has to be greater lay involvement in the MAPPPs, but what shape does that take? How do you select these people? How do you decide if they are representative of the local community? And, above all, how do you ensure that this isn't a kind of Trojan Horse for unchecked dissemination of information about sex offenders which is going to lead to trouble and violence?"

Conclusion

We began this chapter with a quote from the former head of Scotland Yard's Paedophilia Unit, Jim Reynolds, about "lookers" and "doers". We have explored the relationship between the two and suggested that it would be a grave mistake to think that Internet pornography is invariably a sideshow to the main event, which is to prevent the abuse of children in families, schools, clubs and elsewhere by people whom they have reason to trust. We have cited a number of police operations which have ended in the conviction of paedophiles, some of whom have been offending for years. We hope we have also conveyed a certain unease in the world of law enforcement, especially about those perennial concerns priorities and resources. To quote Jim Reynolds again: "You can arrest someone for possession of child abuse images but, to do the job right, you have to look beyond that. You have to ask a number of questions. Who is this person? What are his home circumstances? Does he have kids? Who does he work for? Does he have access to kids through his work? Unfortunately, because of the pressure the police are under, there is often a strong temptation to say 'Look, we haven't got the wherewithal to go the extra mile. Let's send him to court on a charge of possession. Next!' And that's the classic way to miss people who are abusing children."

But, in keeping with the spirit of much of this book, we end on a more positive note. It is no doubt true that some abusers are being missed – and, sadly, as we discussed in Chapter 3, many more do not even reach the criminal justice system. But a conviction for possession of child abuse material is better than no conviction at all – especially since sentences were increased as a result of Operation Cathedral. At least it ensures that the culprit becomes a registered sex offender and, though that, too, is not as central to child protection as many – including the *News of the World* – appear to think, it should not be dismissed as negligible. After all, the police investigating the abduction of eight-year-old Sarah Payne arrived at her murderer Roy Whiting's door within hours of her disappearance. That would not have happened had he not been on the register.

6
Release

I was playing golf recently and I went around with some really nice guys. I thought, "What would they do if they knew who I was?" . . . I don't just want to look at history but also what I can do in the future, for myself and others . . . hurting people is off the agenda, and that's a good feeling.

Released paedophile

This chapter is concerned with what happens when a paedophile has finished his sentence, and leaves prison – in short, what happens to him after his punishment has ended. In particular it follows the story of Phil – not his real name – as he leaves HMP Grendon and attempts to regain a foothold in the community. Shortly after he did so the *News of the World* started its "naming and shaming" policy, and so the community that Phil returned to was even less likely to be welcoming than he might have expected. Even so, as we met with him over the course of two years we were surprised by the difficulties that Phil experienced, and we present perhaps for the first time the various dilemmas and problems faced by a paedophile as he settled initially into a probation hostel, and then moved elsewhere. We outline his attitude towards the community that he was re-entering, and his relationships with the various probation officers whom he encountered; we outline his thoughts about sex and his dilemma of when – or whether – to reveal his offending background to those women with whom he wanted to have a relationship; and we hear of his struggle to find work and maintain his family relationships.

And, after the description has ended, we use Phil's journey to ask some searching questions about the type of society we are in danger of becoming if moral panics replace proper debate, and we place all of this in a broader criminological context at the conclusion of the chapter. In particular, we see through Phil the impossibility of ever "losing" the label paedophile, and as such question whether there is ever any true release for a paedophile. However, it should be stressed that we did not interview Phil with a predetermined set of research questions. Rather, we allowed him to teach us about the world that he was encountering, and to push us in directions that we had hitherto not considered. It was Phil who generated the theoretical context of this chapter, and as a result there emerges a very detailed and troubling picture of Britain in the grip of a moral panic, from the standpoint of a person who was a focus for that moral panic. As such we encounter Phil's dilemma as to whether or not he should lie about his past publicly, while at the same time having to engage in private with the honesty of therapeutic groups run by the probation service. We begin to see some of his difficulties in establishing relationships with adults – putting into practice what he had learned about "repositioning" his sexual fantasies away from children and onto adults, as he had been taught in the SOTP (see chapter 2) – and, more broadly, we embark on a journey with him to discover when an "offender" truly becomes an "ex-offender".

This is not to imply that everything that Phil told us was taken at face value – we were not necessarily on "his side". The story that emerges from him was checked where it could be by using official documentation and printed materials, and through informal discussions with some professionals involved with his case. More importantly, we had the benefit of being able to interview Phil over a long period of time and to observe him in various social settings. Thus, quite apart from formal interviews – which were taped and transcribed – we saw Phil speak at two conferences organized by a national criminal justice charity, and we had the opportunity to socialize with him on several occasions. In doing so we felt that we were able to check, recheck and cross-check information that he provided, so that in the end a detailed and consistent picture could emerge. Of note, the first year's interviews with Phil were presented in an academic context – to the Hostel's 2000 Conference in Liverpool, organized by the Cambridge University Board of Continuing Education, which similarly allowed us to explore the picture that emerged in greater detail.

Obviously ethical considerations were at the heart of our relationship with Phil, and it is perhaps worth presenting these in some detail. Contact with Phil was originally made while he was a serving prisoner at HMP Grendon, and was re-established after he had been released from the prison. As is so often the case in research, this contact was more by chance than by design, and as such we are not trying to suggest that Phil is in some way a "typical" paedophile or sex offender. In some ways it was a "happy coincidence" that we met Phil, and that he was prepared to speak to us. The nature of the research was explained both within the prison and then again after his release, and care was taken to establish that Phil gave "informed consent" for the interviews to proceed. This, we hope, was a two-way process. For ourselves, from the outset, we made it clear to Phil that if we felt that during the course of our conversations he revealed that he was still offending then we would report that matter to the police. This seems like a dramatic step to take – and one that would obviously put pressure on the relationship that we hoped to develop with Phil – but we nonetheless felt that it was a necessary first step in establishing an ethical relationship. We could befriend and advise, but we would not collude with offending, and we had to make that clear. Secondly, we did not pay for any interviews, although on one or two occasions we bought meals and drinks. This might seem unfair, especially as we would benefit financially from the relationship with Phil. However, payment seems to bring with it expectations – in short, that the person being paid has to "sing for his supper", and might therefore be encouraged to embellish details so as to provide the information that the payer "wants". This was of no interest to us, and thankfully Phil did not ask for payment. However, we readily agreed to one of his stipulations – that his identity should not be revealed. Given Phil's circumstances, we clearly would have potentially put him in some danger if we had openly discussed his offending history, and we have continued to protect his identity. This is no simple matter, for obviously we have also had to ensure that the circumstances which he describes are presented in such a way that we do not reveal specific locations, people, situations or events which would by default reveal his identity.

All of this might seem unproblematic. Yet nothing could be further from the truth, and perhaps just one of the ethical dilemmas that we have faced in getting Phil's story into print might reveal something of these difficulties. At one of the conferences that Phil was invited to address, a member of the audience asked what he had been convicted of, given that he was describing his prison experiences. Phil lied, and replied that he had been convicted of property offences – an interesting allusion to the "nick hierarchy" we describe in chapter 4. This seemed to satisfy the audience that Phil was essentially "OK", and we watched as several members of the audience approached him with invitations to come and address their conference, group, school or university. We asked Phil why he had lied, and he explained that he simply couldn't face telling the truth at that point – the *News of the World*'s campaign was at its height – and he had anyway no intention of following up on any offer which had been made. This seemed plausible enough at the most immediate level, but was very unsatisfactory in all sorts of other ways, not least because it revealed Phil's willingness to lie when the circumstances suited. Perhaps we too had been lied to, but, more importantly, an opportunity had been lost to engage with an audience about an issue that Phil was uniquely qualified to talk about, and this gave us cause for concern. We spoke to Phil about this, and, while he rightly pointed out that he had to live with the consequences of what he described and we did not, it was gratifying to note that the next time he addressed a conference and was asked the same question, he chose to tell the truth.

This chapter is divided into two main sections. The first describes the part played generally by the probation service when they deal with sex offenders in the community, so as to provide some context for Phil's journey back into the community. As such it should be read in conjunction with earlier chapters which attempted to deconstruct what we mean by offending generally, and sex offending specifically. This section is based on two documents produced by HM Inspectorate of Probation – *Exercising Constant Vigilance: The Role of the Probation Service in Protecting the Public from Sex Offenders* (Home Office, 1998a), and *Delivering an Enhanced Level of Community Supervision: Report of a Thematic Inspection on the Work of Approved Probation and Bail Hostels* (Home Office, 1998b). As has been outlined above, Phil's journey makes up the second and longest section of the chapter, and this has been further divided into three main themes. Finally a short discussion is provided at the end of the chapter which attempts to see Phil's personal journey as merely one part of what the criminologist Stan Cohen (1985) has described as the "dispersal of discipline" in society as a whole.

Sex offenders in the community

In 1998, in a report entitled *Exercising Constant Vigilance* (Home Office, 1998a), HM chief inspector of probation reported on the numbers of sex offenders being supervised by the probation service at the end of 1996. This report looked at the work undertaken with sex offenders by ten probation areas, and overall concluded that the probation service was "successfully developing their assessment and supervision of sex offenders [and] in the large majority of cases, the quality of work undertaken was testimony to skilled and persistent work on the part of probation staff" (Home Office, 1998a: 9). It also provided a detailed statistical breakdown of the numbers of sex offenders being supervised by the probation service and the type of supervision to which they were subject. We provide this information in table 6.1 and table 6.2.

In 1996, there were 9091 sex offenders on the caseload of the probation service, with 4753 of these in the community and 4338 in prison. Sex offenders represented approximately 3 per cent of the total of court orders supervised by the probation service and 9 per cent of the total throughcare caseload. 27 per cent of sex offenders were subject to probation orders and 12 per cent to combination, community service and other orders, and the report comments upon "the surprisingly high number of community service orders made on offenders convicted of sexual offences" (Home Office, 1998a: 12), although it is also acknowledged that these typically involved the less serious offence of indecent exposure. 14 per cent of sex offenders were subject to post-release supervision – such as the type undertaken with Phil – and 48 per cent to pre-release supervision. In all, these figures represented a 27 per cent increase in the number of sex offenders reported to be on the probation service's caseload since 1995, and the growth was attributed to the increase in throughcare cases arising as a result of the extension of post-release supervision following the implementation of the 1991 Criminal Justice Act.

The chief inspector of probation drew particular attention to several "commendable aspects" of the probation service's work with sex offenders. Chief among these were the facts that protecting the public was unambiguously identified as the central purpose of the probation service's work; that there was a general recognition of the distress and harm experienced by victims of sexual abuse;

Table 6.1 Sex offenders by offence type – probation service
caseload, December 1996

	Caseload at end 1996
Rape and attempted rape	958
Unlawful sexual intercourse	94
Indecent assault on a person under sixteen	1946
Indecent assault on a person aged sixteen or over	730
Incest	68
Gross indecency with a child	283
Indecent exposure	1594
Possessing or taking an obscene photo of a child	89
All other sexual offences	3250
Total	**9012**

that probation officers were exercising a "high level of vigilance";
and that the supervision of sex offenders was a high priority –
though they actually represented a small proportion of the total of
the caseloads being managed.

The report also drew attention to the work that was being undertaken by staff in hostels – an issue that was taken up in the same
year in a thematic inspection by the chief inspector (Home Office,
1998b). This report provides some of the background to Phil's
journey in that it describes what was formally meant to happen
in approved probation hostels, and thus affords us a glimpse of
"the official side's" view of what Phil describes. As such the chief
inspector felt that his inspection demonstrated the ability of hostels
to accommodate and work successfully with "some of the most difficult, damaged and potentially dangerous defendants and offenders
within the criminal justice system, in a manner which gave due
regard to public safety" (Home Office, 1998b: 13). This was no
small matter, for at the time of the thematic report the hostel estate
was capable of providing more than 2200 bed spaces in some ninety-
nine hostels. However, approved hostels are intended to provide
accommodation not simply for offenders, and since 1995 they have
had to provide an enhanced level of supervision of residents
as required by the probation service's National Standards for the
Supervision of Offenders in the Community (which had first been

Table 6.2 Sex offenders by supervision type

	Pre-release	Post-release		
Probation order (PO)			1224	
PO with residency requirement			165	
PO with extended requirements for sex offenders			106	
PO with other requirements			936	
Total probation orders			2431	27%
Community service order			548	
Combination order			342	
Supervision and other order			196	
Total other court order			1086	12%
Young offenders' institution detention	160	66		
Adult statutory supervision	3364	590		
Discretionary conditional release		119		
Parole		222		
Sex offenders supervised to full end of sentence	380	107		
Lifer	258	34		
Special hospital discharge		21		
Other statutory throughcare	32	10		
Voluntary aftercare	144	67		
	4338	1236	5574	62%
Total caseload			9091	100%

introduced in 1992 and were revised three years later). In these national standards the purpose of approved hostels was specifically identified as providing an "enhanced level of supervision to enable certain bailees and offenders to remain under supervision in the community" (Home Office, 1998b: 21).

What this "enhanced level of supervision" actually looked like was never made clear in the thematic report, but aspects of practice and a range of programmes and facilities available within or through a hostel placement which might deliver the required level of supervision included:

- high levels of contact between staff and residents as part of a 24-hour supervised regime
- daily/weekly meetings for all residents which focused on the management of the hostel
- constructive activities designed to promote socially acceptable behaviour
- use of CCTV and other security measures
- engagement with community resources and programmes
- regular formal and informal supervision sessions which were offence focused
- regular liaison with appropriate statutory and voluntary organizations, including the police. (Home Office, 1998b: 45–6)

Of course this enhanced level of supervision applied to all those offenders who entered an approved hostel, and not just to sex offenders. Indeed, not all of the hostels which featured in the thematic report were prepared to accept sex offenders; some restricted the numbers they were prepared to admit, and several which had accepted sex offenders refused to admit any more as a result of specific local circumstances. However, profiles of the 1943 residents about whom information was available revealed that 430 (22 per cent) were recorded as being charged with, or having been found guilty of, a sexual offence. Of these, 233 (54 per cent) were bailees, which suggested that the courts did not regard their alleged offences to be so serious as to require being remanded in custody. A further sixty-three (15 per cent) were subject to a probation order with a condition of residence, and 124 (29 per cent) were, like Phil, released prisoners subject to parole or licence which required them to live at a hostel as part of a planned strategy for their reintegration into the community. Overall, the thematic inspection concluded that:

There was convincing evidence that approved hostels were better equipped to manage the risks posed by sex offenders in the community than other community-based arrangements. Those hostels inspected who were accommodating sex offenders demonstrated an ability to provide a constructive, supportive and restrictive regime as part of an enhanced level of supervision. (Home Office, 1998b: 72)

A little over twelve months later Phil would be released from custody and put this conclusion to the test.

Phil's journey – in his own words

We formally interviewed Phil on four separate occasions, with each interview lasting some two hours. These interviews would be described academically as "unstructured" in that they did not follow any set pattern, and that Phil prompted the discussions. Clearly there were areas that we wanted to discuss, but we did not have a set list of questions which would have structured the interview by imposing our world view onto his. He had the power to take the interview in the direction that he wanted it to go, and we as the researchers were being taught by him rather than the other way round. He was our guide, and as such he took us down three different but interconnected roads which make up the themes of this journey. The first was labelled "The hostel is a prison", and on the way we met hostel staff as controllers who acted just like prison officers. Indeed, when he uses descriptions such as these it is clear that the social work ethos that used to characterize the work of the probation service has all but disappeared. The second road was named "Probation officers are 'all style but no fitba'", by which we came to understand that, while they tried to care, probation officers were under so much pressure – of various kinds – that the end result was that Phil simply became another file in an already full cabinet. Finally, the third road was called "Being a sex offender", and this road was perhaps the most dangerous of them all to travel down. It was on this road that we were advised of the hazard of lapses, triggered by a lack of "self-esteem", and of Phil's hopes for the future and his worry that he won't be able to make that future real. For ultimately these roads led to the same place – punishment. Travel with us down these roads, and judge for yourself the landscape that you can see by the road's edge. And when you're there, look beyond that landscape into the distance in space and time, and try to see what type of society we are in danger of becoming.

The hostel is a prison

Phil chose the hostel in which he lived initially from the probation service's list of hostels, and because the town had good railway and road connections which would get him to Scotland – where his family live – and also to London. He remembered the excitement of visiting the hostel for the first time with an officer from HMP Grendon on a pre-release visit. "It was a key day", he commented, especially as finding accommodation for released sex offenders is no simple matter. Indeed, in 1998 the Chartered Institute of Housing was prompted to publish guidance for housing agencies after "some local authorities have responded to concerns about the rehousing of offenders by considering 'blanket bans' to exclude offenders generally, or sex offenders in particular in their allocation policies" (Chartered Institute of Housing, 1998). Yet a recent NACRO report about reducing the risks of reoffending for sex offenders who have been released from jail emphasized the importance of finding sex offenders "stable accommodation" (NACRO, 1998). So Phil was lucky, although he does not always see things that way. His ambivalent views about the hostel are evident in his description of his first impressions.

> The hostel felt clean. The rooms were small. In fact I was quite staggered by some of the rooms, as they were smaller than cells. The hostel wasn't welcoming; the rooms were just so bare. You got the feeling that they didn't want you there long. I wasn't able to paint my walls – I love colour – and I wasn't allowed to bring my budgie. It had a prison feel. I was given a list of rules, and told that I'd be breached for this and for that, and so it came across as a prison without walls. The staff were very keen to tell me that they could search my room, and of course there was an eleven o'clock curfew.

These observations use two of the themes that would run throughout our conversations with Phil. First, that the hostel had a "prison feel", and second, part of that feel was related to the attitudes of the hostel staff. In relation to this first theme, for example, Phil commented that the hostel has got "a huge similarity to prison, and

I just sometimes see it as having a bigger exercise yard – the town. At 2300 you're in your room, and at 0800 they knock and open your door – its just like prison." Similarly, Phil thought that the hostel staff were "not really very different from prison officers", and described their attitude as being "do this, do that, eat now." When pushed about what he meant by this, he maintained that "what seems to be important to them is that you're in your room at 2300 and out at 0800, and in some cases they just barge in. It's a head-count mentality really – just like in prison." For Phil this issue of "barging in" was very important, as it not only impinged on his privacy, but thus also his right to be seen as an individual, and an equal. "Some of the staff just haven't got the measure of the importance of privacy and your own space. It's like always having a video camera on – you're controlled."

This theme of the hostel as a prison was further amplified by Phil's fellow hostellers, as it meant that there was "a lot of prison speak – down on the staff; fucking rules; they're all a load of wankers". Many of the younger residents are drug users, and Phil describes retiring to his room where he had his "wee telly" almost as if he was describing his technique for surviving in prison. Nonetheless "there were incidents . . . I'd complain about the noise and the smell of marijuana all over the place", and so clearly the idea that the staff were all jailers with omnipotent controlling powers had limits, and indeed Phil himself recognized this. He commented that "they have the rules, but they don't police them", and he believed that this was the case because they are "understaffed and overworked". This worried him, especially as his recent experiences at HMP Grendon had encouraged him to believe that community rules were important, and that group meetings were an appropriate way of reconciling differences. Yet, "the meetings in the hostel are so poorly put together . . . people drop in and out, so the staff are controlling in relation to what they say are the rules – they can be quite strong about incidentals, like our wee cleaning jobs – but the important rules about people interacting they are less strong with . . . it's an anomaly. In Grendon you just didn't get away with things." In short, for Phil, hostel staff fail on two different levels – "they have the rules, but they don't police them", and "they want to care but they don't know how to." Indeed, the observation that "at Grendon you just didn't get away with things" is indicative of his belief that his "change", or more simply what he attributes to staying out of trouble, can be laid at the door of HMP Grendon – "my change is

85 per cent Grendon and 15 per cent the hostel's . . . Grendon's was the massive contribution."

Probation officers are "all style but no fitba"

Phil had had a variety of probation officers (POs) – from POs seconded to work within prisons to those who supervised him in the community and ran sex offender treatment groups. Again reflecting an earlier theme, the seconded PO at HMP Grendon seems to have been the one person who Phil felt "listened to him", even if she "didn't deliver". These two issues, of being listened to and the delivery of the service that probation provided, remained the consistent themes throughout our discussions. A good example of both themes emerging within the one conversation arose when Phil described his sex offender treatment group that was run on a Monday by a PO.

> It's not very helpful. In fact it's slowly dismantling the work that I did at Grendon. There you sat around and talked, and shared and challenged about your offending. On Monday night a female PO chairs a two-hour meeting and she talks for one and a half hours. It's a nodding process with us listening. If we say what she's thinking we get a brownie point. We have to think as she does. But we should be talking and challenging – I know this is scathing, but what I'm saying is anonymous . . . The woman seems to have a personal agenda, and I understand how hard it is to cope with your personal feelings, but I just seem to be being told that I'm being controlled – a person in authority is controlling me, and then I try and talk about my offence and it gives me great pain.

Of note – and something that we'll discuss when we look at Phil's history of offending – it should be acknowledged that all of the POs with whom he has dealt are female, and this clearly forms part of the unspoken context within which he discusses these issues. Nonetheless this conjures up a picture of Phil being controlled and managed, rather than being helped in any therapeutic way. "We have to think as she does" is a very powerful statement, and having made it Phil almost immediately sought reassurance that the interview would be confidential, which conveys some measure of that power as he sees it. He later explains that he thinks that POs have a "functioning and managing role"; that "it's like they are trying to manage you rather than getting to know you"; and "at times it's clear that they are just getting through the day." What comes across to

Phil is that the POs are trying to say "'I'm in charge' . . . knocking you around and showing you that you'll get into trouble because they're the boss." The effect of all this was "you're a file in a cabinet that they take out, and put back in again after they've seen you . . . you're a number."

Phil thought that "people go into probation because they care", but that they change in time "because they get abused". Part of the reason for that change was their "massive case load", which Phil maintained was "all they wanted to talk about". He went further, and commented that the POs that he'd worked with were "people with problems and they seem to want to share their problems . . . they're stressed, they function, and all of them seem to look at their watches." Indeed, the PO to whom he had originally been assigned had had to take time off because of stress. "They want to care, but they find it hard to find that piece of ground that will let them care", which led Phil to use an old Scottish footballing phrase, that the POs had "bags of style, but no fitba". In other words that they had style and flair, but ultimately they lost the game because they couldn't score any goals. His conclusion was: "It's a wonderful idea, the probation service, but I think that as an organization they're all insecure because of the government."

Being a sex offender

Much of what Phil discusses is intimately bound up with his status as someone who has committed sex offences. His current conviction is his second for indecent assault on girls, and, as has previously been alluded to, some of the difficulties that he has with his probation officers are linked to the idea of women controlling him, as opposed to his controlling women – or girls. As a sex offender, Phil was obliged to register with the local police – a process that he described as "no big deal, in fact I think they were quite embarrassed" – and he had to reside in the hostel. Similarly, he could change his residence only with the agreement of his probation officer, and "I couldn't go within 10 miles of my victims, and couldn't work where there were children."

Phil describes "working hard at Grendon about the nature of my offence", and recounts the difficulties he has keeping the momentum of this progress going since leaving prison. In particular, believing that he has to lie in public about the nature of his offence troubles him, especially as this makes him "always feel that I had to look over my shoulder." He explains that much of his offending is linked to the relationship that he had had as a child with his mother, but that he learned to accept responsibility for his offences while at HMP Grendon. "I learned at Grendon to become an adult, having been a child. I learned to accept responsibility." Part of this was achieved through psychodrama, which Phil describes as unlocking him "from darkness". "My control had been taken away from me in childhood, and I tried to regain my control by sexually abusing young girls." Thus issues related to status, responsibility, self-esteem and being treated as an equal are central to the understanding that Phil has of why he has offended and what he can do about that offending behaviour, and thus colour his views of the hostel and probation staff. "I went to the hostel and was treated as a child again, with all that taken away from me."

This statement obviously alludes to a lapse that Phil had while living in the hostel, although it also suggests that he believes that others should take the blame rather than he himself. This lapse is of interest from many perspectives, and so we will spend a little time using Phil's voice outlining what occurred.

> I felt increasingly frustrated sexually. I was doing my best, and I was attracted to adult women and so I started looking in newspaper personals. I started to groom a friend to let me look at personals on the Internet, and I picked out one that would allow me to have [sex – describes a specific sexual encounter]. Through a bizarre set of circumstances [describes a specific set of circumstances] . . . the balloon went up. I spoke about the issue on relapse. It was like a can of petrol to the woman who runs the course – fair do's, as she was right to be angry. The PO asked why I hadn't gone into a phone box and got a number that way. I think that it freaked them that I had done it on the Internet. It was a serious lapse, but it was with adult women, and my coping strategies for not abusing children is intact.

There are at least three issues here which are worthy of further consideration. First is the whole question of sex, and how Phil is expected to deal with his sexual needs. Second, the passage makes us consider how well this lapse was dealt with by those who were responsible for supervising him within the community, and finally it reminds us of the problems experienced by prisoners who have been released back into the community, and who are trying to create a new start for themselves. Space does not allow for each of these themes to be pursued extensively, and for the purpose of this chapter it is perhaps of greater interest to consider the first issue identified – namely, and using Phil's words, what he is supposed to do when he becomes "increasingly frustrated sexually". This is a serious question, and one that needs to be considered on several levels. How does he establish relationships with women, given what he has done? Should he be honest about his past, and risk rejection? Is his only alternative to find prostitutes advertised in the local phone box? Indeed, is he encouraged to talk about sex at all, or is this an issue that is so emotionally charged that it is simply best avoided?

Phil provides his own answers to these questions, some of which echo one of the author's recollections of having set up a sex offender treatment programme within a prison setting (Wilson, 1990). He states, quite simply, "I'm not allowed to talk about sex", which might also explain the dynamics of his treatment group, which he has described as a "nodding process with us listening". He goes on: "they do want us to have a relationship, but it's all 'roses over the cottage door' . . . it's simply not a realistic picture." He further explains that his curfew impinges on his being able to meet women at a pub or club as he has to be back in the hostel by 2300 hours. "How can I talk to a lady when I'm looking at the clock? I'm Cinderella." In some senses these observations are a way of excusing his lapse. For example, he maintains that, instead of going through the difficulties of trying to establish a relationship, "I thought that a fleeting, passing, sexual situation would be better." Yet this statement rather supports his PO's question of why he hadn't just found a prostitute's number in a telephone box, and clearly more was at stake than he is prepared to admit. After all, why the specific type of sexual encounter he attempted to create, and what significance should we give to his use of the phrase "grooming a friend" – which echoes the process that many sex offenders engage in with their victims – to allow him to use the Internet? Nonetheless, some of his behaviour is explicable in relation to his need for self-esteem, and the relationship that he had had as a child with his mother. In short, "if I have an adult relationship and that goes pear-shaped for me, that's high risk."

This is a complex picture, and the analysis provided is not meant to be definitive. However, what is also significant is the predicament that he finds himself in as an offender generally, and as a sexual offender and paedophile specifically. He wants to put the past behind him; he wants to change his status as an offender and find a new way of living, but how does he do that? Twenty years ago, being released from prison would have allowed him to have re-entered the community as a "free man", for when he moved beyond the prison's walls – the very visible boundary to punishment – his punishment had ended. Now the boundaries to punishment have become invisible, and the community has begun to serve the same function as the jail. Indeed, some insight into his predicament can be gleaned by his simple description of playing golf. "I was playing golf recently and I went around with some really nice guys. I thought, 'What would they do if they knew who I was?' We open up about what we've done, but what can we do then? I don't just want to look at history but also what I can do in the future, for myself and others . . . hurting people is off the agenda, and that's a good feeling."

Here he is asking us to accept that he has changed his ways, but recognizes that to explain what he has done will merely alienate him further from those by whom he wants to be accepted. His punishment has not ended, merely moved into new territories. And while punishment had been confined within prison, with all its rules, procedures and boundaries, Phil knew where things stood – something which also partly explains his obvious love of HMP Grendon. Released back into the community, Phil finds himself confused and lost, and being punished yet again. He amplifies this thought in his description of how he believes he is seen by the public – that is, if the public knew that he had been a paedophile. "People are not prepared to accept that there are folk like me who get it wrong in a big way. They don't want to know me – I don't exist. People are asking me to become invisible. I'm their worst nightmare. My self-esteem levels are very low, and I feel like a piece of shit. That's a trigger for me, but I'm not going to offend again. I've been a nasty man, but I know I can be a person of worth. I have changed, and I know I can give something back."

Discussion

Phil's journey is but one of a number of journeys being undertaken by offenders generally, and sex offenders specifically. Perhaps some might argue that it is right and proper that the circumstances that released offenders encounter should be as tough as possible, although it is our view that this will make it harder – not simpler – to protect our children and prevent reoffending, a theme at the very heart of this book. And, just as importantly, we argue that this type of thinking – if it becomes public policy – will ultimately and fundamentally alter the very fabric of our society. For, in following Phil's journey, and perhaps unfairly generalizing from it, we felt that we were witnessing first hand Cohen's (1985) vision of social control and the "dispersal of discipline", and what Foucault (1977) has described as the "carceral society". In such a society, punishment is no longer simply a device for altering an individual's behaviour, but rather becomes the basis on which the physical and social structures of the whole of society are created. In short, punishment doesn't simply happen to offenders within a prison, but ultimately happens everywhere and affects us all. So, for Foucault, "carceral impulses" swarmed outside of prison – from "closed" to "open" sites – and thus infected schools, hospitals and factories, and where the powerful inspected and kept watch over the powerless.

While we see Foucault as a poetic influence on our thinking about Phil and his journey, our main academic debt is to Stan Cohen. And while it has to be remembered that Cohen wrote before the great penal expansion of 1993 – prompted by the murder of James Bulger (c.f. Wilson and Ashton, 1998) – the ideas that he sets out are worth reconsidering. For what Cohen (1985: 83–4) describes is the future of punishment, as he saw it at the time, being based upon a "gradual expansion and intensification of the system; a dispersal of its mechanisms from more closed to more open sites and a consequent increase in the invisibility of social control and the degree of its penetration into the social body." As such he questioned where the prison ends and the community begins, and tried to establish whether alternatives to custody were in fact any different from "the real thing". Cohen wanted to know about what was going on inside the punishment machine and whether punishment in the community was any less "intrusive, onerous, coercive, stigmatising, artificial and bureaucratic; more humane, just, fair, helpful, natural and informal" (Cohen, 1985: 69). He tried to do this by looking at questions related to the size and density of the system; its identity and visibility – "what does the object look like and what are its boundaries?"; and at the issue of penetration. In short, how the dispersal of punishment affected its "surrounding space" – where all of us live.

For Cohen was interested not just in the expansion of the system, but also in the intensity of punishment when it escaped over the prison's walls. In these circumstances, is the prisoner being punished twice? Once in the prison and then again after release into the

123

community, but this time by a new group of experts working in a different setting? This might or might not be the case, but Cohen was also clear that those institutions involved in punishment have to struggle for survival, and that "the struggle is an unequal one: the old guard – the police, judges, prosecutors, custodial staff – remain the most powerful actors in the system. They are the ones that define, that call the tune. All the others – the forces of progress and reform – have to make deals, compromises and trade-offs in order to make a few gains" (Cohen, 1985: 95).

We've tried to use Phil's voice to look inside the punishment machine – the carceral archipelago – to see if, in the words of Stan Cohen, it is less "intrusive, onerous and coercive". Phil would not see it as such, but instead would present us with his predicament. For him punishment hasn't just moved location, but has got even more intense. "It's like always having a video camera on", he tells us, and the key word here is "always". There is no respite; no escape. The staff don't wear uniforms and carry keys, and are called by different names within another hierarchy, but the end effect is that he is still told to "do this, do that, eat now." Control comes in a variety of forms – especially in the wake of the Prison–Probation Review, and can be masked in any number of ways, but the end product is still control. We've also tried to use Phil's observations to see if they foretell of more general trends within punishment – if they are the shape of things to come not just for probation and hostels and for "punishment in the community", but also for what that community might be like to live and work in.

In our final informal interview with Phil – snatched before his appearance at yet another conference, we returned to several of the themes that we had pursued with him on his journey from prison to the community, on the road from offender to "non-offender", and in his case from paedophile to someone interested in sexual relations with adults. Indeed, the issue of sex became central to this final interview as Phil became increasingly open about his sexual feelings. "How are you going to cope?" we asked, to which Phil gave some thought before replying not in words, but in actions. "Like this", he said, and motioned with his hand the gesture for masturbation the world over. That was hardly the best place to stop our interview, but with that he was off, and since then we have all but lost contact.

7

Communities in Need of "Community Notification"?

A lot of the people who protested were not representative of the community. They were what you might call the "alienated within".
Father Gary Waddington, parish priest, Paulsgrove estate

Introduction

In the summer of 2000, a place called Paulsgrove in Portsmouth grabbed the fifteen-minutes' worth of fame which is our apparent birthright in this media age. During the first heady week of August, the cameras of national and international broadcasters recorded some bizarre images. A four-year-old child clutching a bag of sweets in one hand and a placard in the other, saying: "Kill the paedophiles. In it." Shaven-headed teenagers linking arms with twenty- and thirty-something mums to sing: "You'll Never Walk Alone". The sound of stones hurled through front-room windows and the smell of torched cars.

Newspaper pundits raided the lexicon of parallels, contemporary and ancient, to try to explain what was happening. The ethnic cleansing of Bosnia. The anti-Jewish savagery of *Kristallnacht* in 1938. The hysteria over witchcraft in seventeenth-century Salem. All were invoked. On daytime TV and late-night radio phone-ins, the airwaves throbbed with amateur psychology and instant analysis.

Amid the welter of strident opinion, one view quickly came to the fore: that something nasty and illiberal had been uncorked on the south coast and that "hang 'em high" vigilantism was alien to the

125

British way of protest. In the newspapers, unflattering profiles of the "ring-leaders" began to appear, and Paulsgrove found itself installed in the hall of infamy reserved for other troubled estates of the last decade, such as Blackbird Leys in Oxford and Meadow Well in North Shields. Thus condemned and pigeon-holed, they return to the obscurity from whence they came. Case closed.

Except that Paulsgrove is different. Yes, it was about paedophiles. But it was about much more than that. Indeed, it reflects all of the issues which this book seeks to address: the mistaken idea that communities are safer when the "dirty old men" are driven out; the repercussions of failing to confront child sex abuse within families; the perceived indifference of officialdom to local concerns.

It was also about the powerlessness of those whose voice is seldom heard unless they shout from the rooftops and smash a few slates in the process. In other words, it was very much a working-class protest. To understand how much this shaped events, later in this chapter we look at another anti-paedophile campaign, at Tooting, in a well-heeled part of south London. The comparison is illuminating.

"The monstrous regiment of women"

Katrina Kessell, the moving force behind Residents Against Paedophiles (RAP), is perched on a sofa which has seen better days, surrounded by press cuttings and a mass of other paperwork. On the wall is a photo of her and four of her five children (the eldest, a boy aged seventeen, lives with her mother). Two of the chairs in the draughty front room are broken. A window is cracked.

She favours sweatshirts with logos and her red hair is slicked into a coxcomb. She looks like she can take care of herself in a tight corner. But, apart from a truculent glare with which she sees off one of her daughters who has wandered in whining, this is a very different Katrina from the harridan of press reports – the Katrina who was fined £60 by the magistrates court for, as she puts it, "shouting me mouth off in the street". Today she is willing to reflect calmly, for the most part, on what happened, and is able to surprise as well.

We start by talking about the pre-August 2000 history of Paulsgrove. She says that, for at least eighteen months, residents had expressed concern about paedophiles on the estate. And that a petition with 500 to 600 names had been presented to Portsmouth City

Council calling for Victor Burnett, a convicted sex offender, who was to become the first "victim" of the rioting, to be moved out. (It is worth noting here that the local MP, Syd Rapson – who also lives on the estate – could not recall any discussion about paedophiles prior to August 2000 nor, at that time, had he heard of the name Victor Burnett. More of that later.)

Victor Burnett lived near the community centre and within yards of a school. He had spent more than fourteen of his fifty-six years in jail for sex offences. By his own admission, he had abused up to forty children between the ages of eleven and fifteen. And neither electric shock treatment nor a course of female hormone injections had curbed his instincts. Burnett had not been arrested since being released from Maidstone Prison in 1994, but Kessell and others believe that, for more than a year before August 2000, he was "grooming" local children in preparation for further offences: "At the beginning, we didn't know that he'd done time or that he'd been driven out of an area of London because of his crimes. What worried parents here was his behaviour. He was befriending kids. Inviting them into his flat. Giving them sweets." Another estate resident fuelled the unease by reporting that Burnett had been seen wearing shorts.

So, what was the council's response to the petition? "Burnett was moved out for a day. They fireproofed his front door and moved him back again. End of story." It wasn't the whole story, though, because the police were monitoring Burnett. Some council officials knew that, but the residents did not. However, despite the abortive petition to the council, even Katrina Kessell admits that paedophiles were hardly a "burning issue" on Paulsgrove before the summer of 2000. One story sums up the almost casual attitude towards them, a far cry from the hysteria which later engulfed the estate. She says there were quite a few paedophiles whom residents "knew of" ("knew" as in taproom gossip and innuendo rather than incontrovertible fact – but that's by the by): "Listen, this is a close-knit community. People know of things which went on years ago. There's a man here who committed a paedophile offence in 1976. He's still on the estate and once, when my son fell over in the street and cut his knee, this chap pretended to be a doctor and tried to get my boy to come into his house. But I'd warned him about the bloke and the lad just told him to get lost."

It sounds like the sort of encounter that parents down the years have prepared their children for and which ends with no lasting harm done. Then she adds revealingly: "Trouble is, you don't know what a paedophile looks like now. They can come out of the wood-work from anywhere."

That's a thought-provoking statement – a statement with layers of meaning. It could suggest the fantastic idea that, somehow, the paedophile who once upon a time was easy to identify as the slimeball in the mucky mac has transmogrified into Everyman (or perhaps every-insect). Equally, it could be expressing awareness that the paedophile has no distinguishing features, no devil's hoof – an eminently sensible view which would do more to promote child protection than some of the grotesque caricatures peddled in the tabloids.

This is of more than semantic interest. It is the kind of confused and confusing sentiment which affects the way people lead their lives. Another active member of Paulsgrove's Residents Against Pae-dophiles is Michelle Smith, who has five children. She put it like this: "I'm not paranoid, I'm not a trouble-maker, I'm a mum and I will protect my children with my life. And if I can prevent anything happening to my kids, I'll do it. If that means not going to the park because I don't know who's going to be hiding in the bushes, they don't go to the park. Sorted."

After saying that, with real passion in her voice, she rushed into the kitchen and sobbed for several minutes. But why such intense emotion when no children have been sexually assaulted in that park and the biggest scare seems to have been an unidentified man taking photos outside a school? Because she, like Katrina Kessell, was abused as a child and has never really dealt with all of the consequences: "When I was growing up, you never heard about all this paedophile stuff. Nobody listened to children – and nobody really talked any-way. And it's because we didn't talk about it thirty years ago that it's a bigger problem now."

She's not alone in that judgement. Indeed, there are many other "victims" on Paulsgrove – far more than you might expect to find in a concentrated area – who feel the same way. This, perhaps more than anything, is the clue to the violence which erupted in August 2000.

Stories from the frontline

Three spiky, opinionated women are sitting in the front room of a house in Winchcombe Road on the Paulsgrove estate. They are

128

all smoking heavily, and children of various ages and sizes drift in and out of the fug. The house belongs to Sharon Mills, the oldest of the three, who has four grown-up children and fifteen grandchildren. Her companions are Julie Waldram and Michelle Smith.

Sharon: "I've got people in my own family who were abused, and I know a woman of sixty on this estate who has only just admitted that she was abused as a child. That was a direct result of what went off in August 2000. You don't go through nine months of hell having a child to have them fucking abused."

Michelle: "The man who done it to me is dead, thank Christ. Yeh, been there, done that, wore the tee-shirt. As far as I'm concerned, a paedophile will never change. They may have treatment, therapy, whatever they call it, but you can't change their nature. Why can't they just fry part of their brain? Or, better still, just chop it off – mind you, then they would just use something else."

Julie (who has a boy of five and a girl of nine): " It's more the physical and mental abuse which made an impact on me. I've blocked out the sexual side." Not faced up to, but blocked out. And the consequence? "For me, you can't trust no one these days. Not the church, no one. I'm terrified of the paedophile problem. And I'm stopping my own kids having a life."

Stories from the "front line" – whether it's war abroad or sex abuse at home – can be problematic. It's all too easy to inflate a few snapshots into a plausible strategic picture, which may, on closer inspection, turn out to be badly flawed. But all of the available evidence about Paulsgrove points in the same direction. It is an estate with a high degree of social problems, many of them revolving around large families, disaffected youngsters (40 per cent of the 16,000 population is under sixteen), domestic and sexual abuse and a strong feeling of alienation.

Paulsgrove, and the adjoining area, Wymering, were built as slum-clearance estates. Wymering was begun as a "Garden City" just before the Second World War. Paulsgrove went up in the 1950s, during the Macmillan heyday of public housing. The two estates squat above Portsmouth, physically cut off from it by the Southampton Road and the M27, and psychologically isolated too. There is only one road into Paulsgrove, Allaway Avenue, and, despite the absence of tower blocks and the many green spaces, it feels like some kind of beleaguered enclave, with a completely different persona from Portsea Island and Southsea, the "true" Portsmouth.

Father Gary Waddington is the vicar of Paulsgrove. His unattractive, modernist church, St Michael and All Angels, overlooks Allaway Avenue and the second-floor flat once occupied by Victor Burnett, so he had a bird's-eye view of what happened in 2000 and the social backcloth to it: "The attitude in Portsmouth towards Paulsgrove is that it's the place where all the problem families, all those nasty people, the great unwashed, are shipped out to. Deported if you like. So, not surprisingly, many of the residents here suffer from low esteem. And they think that because they live here they have to shout to be heard." Father Gary is young and wears fashionable black denims and his dark hair is gelled. He is highly articulate and his deliberate choice of language – with its emphasis on alienation – has striking echoes of the sentiments expressed by some of the estate mothers about physically isolating paedophiles.

Michelle Smith: "There's got to be somewhere they can put paedophiles, away from the community."

Julie Waldram: "What about the fort in the Solent? On No-Man's Island. Ship the scumbags out there."

Katrina Kessell: "Years ago, they had these Pestalozzi villages. They were special places for children, with high walls around them. They were little communities and everything they needed was on the inside. I reckon there should be special villages for convicted paedophiles. If their families want to stick by them, they can live there too."

It's all too easy, of course, to point up the inconsistency in such sentiments – in casting the paedophile as an alien "other", beyond the pale of decent society. After all, these are the same women who have been sexually abused by grandfathers and step-parents and who accept, when pressed, that the most insidious enemy lies within families, not lurking outside. However, in talking of deporting paedophiles to islands or barricading them behind high walls, are they not borrowing from the same vocabulary as those urban planners who decreed that problem families should be dumped on isolated estates – estates like Paulsgrove?

Gill Mackenzie had a crash course in the dynamics of the protest during those turbulent days of August. Until her retirement in 2001, she was the spokesperson on sex offender issues for the Association of Chief Officers of Probation. A hugely respected figure, both in Gloucestershire where she worked and on the national stage, she found herself arguing the case for sanity and moderation against

130

the twin assaults from Wapping (the *News of the World*) and Paulsgrove:

> Naturally, we were horrified at what was going on there. The violence and the vigilantism. And, of course, it was driving paedophiles underground, so *increasing* the risk to public safety. But that's not to say the women of Paulsgrove didn't have a point. Victor Burnett had been placed right in the middle of the estate, close to a school. That was hardly a sensible decision.
>
> And you also have to say that, from the women's point of view, the council appeared to be displaying an authoritarian, middle-class and *male* attitude.
>
> Remember, all the key players from the "authority" side were men: the director of social services, the chief probation officer, the local police superintendent. And the women protesting had been let down and betrayed many times in their personal lives by men, so I think this also helped put their backs up.

Syd Rapson was a local councillor for thirty years before winning the Westminster seat of Portsmouth North:

> I still have a great deal of sympathy for some of the people involved in the trouble. They just wanted to make the place safer for their children. OK, this is a council estate [though now with more than 50 per cent owner occupation] and the only area with a substantial stock of welfare housing, but people feel that's no reason why we should bear the pain of having paedophiles relocated here. Or be a dustbin for other social problems.
>
> Although I'm a level-headed MP, the thought of clearing the estate of paedophiles, potentially dangerous people, was welcome – even though I knew they would go somewhere else and become someone else's problem. So I have to admit that there is a certain satisfaction in saying, "well, something good did come out of the trouble in August 2000."

What were the good things to come out of it? "Children are more aware of the paedophile problem now. And parents too are being educated in organized sessions on appropriate advice to give to their kids about sex offenders." Then a pause – as though admitting that he's putting too optimistic a gloss on things. "But yes, there is still an underlying fear that they are amongst us – and they are."

The MP's story

It's worth exploring in a little more detail Syd Rapson's views. First, because, as we shall see, they don't entirely hang together. And second, because his role in the events of August 2000 was not that of a mere bystander. Indeed, he came perilously close to being attacked himself and saw his next-door neighbour's house firebombed. After that incident, an anonymous caller told him: "We made a mistake. It should have been your gaff."

Syd Rapson is fifty-nine, a former aircraft fitter and part of the generation of Paulsgrove pioneers known as Grovers. He's working-class Labour to his fingertips, and if anyone can instinctively articulate the concerns of his constituents, he should be able to. But for a few days in that first week of August 2000, he found himself struggling against the maelstrom. And like some of the national commentators, he, too, reaches for lurid parallels to explain his sense of shock:

> When the mob was approaching along this road [Washbrook Road], at first all you could hear was a low murmur. Then it began to rise until you could make out screaming and particular slogans being shouted. I tell you, it was like a scene from a Frankenstein film. It was terrifying.

Then, switching analogies:

> It made me realize how the Nazis murdered Jews who were their neighbours. After all, these were people I knew, who I'd had a drink with, and now they wanted to kill. If I'd been in their way, they would have killed me.

Syd Rapson vigorously disputes the claim made by Katrina Kessell that the trouble was borne out of frustration at the council's failure to address the paedophile problem on the estate over the previous eighteen months:

> I can tell you the issue was never raised with local councillors. Nor in my weekly surgeries. It's true that matters of sex or abuse came up – especially when people were giving a reason for wanting to be rehoused. They might mention incest, domestic violence, that kind of thing. But the word "paedophile" was virtually unknown here.

132

And what about Victor Burnett?

> Katrina Kessell only found out about Burnett towards the end of July 2000. It's simply not true that his name had been raised before that with the council. I've checked with them and they knew nothing about him. The only person who did was the director of social services, Rob Hutchinson, and that's because he was in close contact with the police.

And Syd Rapson's version, rather than Katrina Kessell's, is supported by a comment from her fellow protester Sharon Mills, who, incidentally, is no friend of the MP: "It was when I saw Victor Burnett's picture in the *News of the World* that it clicked. He was the guy who had been trying to take my nephew under his wing." Would she have put it like that if Burnett's name had been a local byword for deviant behaviour for a full eighteen months or so?

So, if the explosion of anger in August cannot be sourced to a slow-burning fuse of disquiet over the rehousing of paedophiles, where else should we look for the spark? Syd Rapson identifies three causes – two particular to Paulsgrove and one which has laid the foundation for many a summer riot.

Cause one. "This is an estate with a history of people sorting out problems with their own hands if necessary. We had a case of a local petty criminal, a 'likeable rogue', who had a bit too much to drink one night, got into an argument outside the pub with some fellows and was kicked to death in the street. On one of the roads here, there are four or five families who are all related. If you upset one, you upset them all – and that can mean serious trouble. It's like the old East End of London."

Cause two. "I think people were targeting paedophiles to distract attention from the sex abuse which goes on within families here. It was a way of assuaging their own guilt. One woman who joined the mob has a son who had been arrested for sexual assault. But she said: 'Oh, that's different, he's not guilty – and he's not a paedophile.'"

(There was also a case of a convicted paedophile who joined the marchers and signed their petition. What better place to hide than among the mob?)

Cause three. "Remember the time of year – and the weather. First week of August and the schools had broken up. Teenagers on the streets. Long, hot nights – people drinking outside pubs till late. How many riots have we seen erupt in the summer in those sort of circumstances?"

That all makes sense, and the second of the causes seems to have a universal ring of plausibility which may be applied more generally to contemporary society's concern/obsession with paedophiles. But remember Syd Rapson's earlier comments about ridding the estate of paedophiles who had been imported from elsewhere. Now they appear more like the self-serving response of a politician anxious to appease his constituents than convictions genuinely held. As does his reported comment to the *Daily Telegraph* on 10 August, 2000: "This is a lovely estate with good housing and well-motivated people and this one incident has brought them notoriety."

In the smoky front lounge of Sharon Mills's house, mention of Syd Rapson's name provokes hoots of derision: "He's not for his people. He's full of shit. God knows what he really thinks."

Perhaps every MP needs to be able to face in two (or more) directions at once. An MP who has reason to fear for his life, even more so. And Syd Rapson was certainly in some danger. "One night, after the pubs closed, I was tipped off that the mob was coming for me. We moved pretty sharpish. I was put in the back of a car and smuggled out of the estate. Luckily, my wife, Phyllis, was away at the time."

Nor was it the only occasion that cloak-and-dagger measures helped frustrate the vigilantes. When a restless crowd surrounded the home of a suspected paedophile, three police officers went inside, one carrying a large holdall. Thirty minutes later, four men in police uniform emerged and drove off in a waiting van. It was well clear of Paulsgrove before the mob realized that one of the "officers" was the target of their hate, kitted out as a member of the Hampshire constabulary.

Who speaks for the community?

In the past twenty years or so, few words have been more casually used and abused than "community". Whether the issue is race relations, the environmental impact of heavy lorries or school closures, the interests of the local "community" are invoked to validate a course of action. Consider how many times news programmes on radio and television quote a "community spokesperson".

But what on earth does it mean? If it is intended to suggest that on every noteworthy issue there is a homogeneous group of people whose interests coincide, that is clearly rubbish. Is there a black community? Or a gay community? No. There are people who may share a skin colour or sexual orientation but who are as different in politics, temperament and lifestyle as Osama Bin Laden and George W. Bush.

Applying that rule of thumb to "community disclosure", which is at the heart of this book, one has to ask: which community is it whose interests are to be served by disclosing the names, addresses and photographs of convicted paedophiles living among them? *News of the World* executives would presumably have no difficulty in answering that question. It is the decent, wholesome families who make up the bulk of its readership and who are being cruelly betrayed by politicians, the courts, and the liberal chattering classes.

But what of those who don't live in a tabloid never-never land? Take Paulsgrove, for example, with its many dysfunctional families and its social problems. Even in normal times, trying to identify the "community" is as rewarding as counting grains of sand. Under the pressure of the events of August 2000, it becomes impossible.

Let's take, as our starting-point, Syd Rapson. After all, an MP, though not mandated on specific issues, unlike a delegate, is expected to represent the broad views of his constituency. What does he think of "community disclosure"?

"First of all, I have no idea how many paedophiles are living here. And I have no wish to know. I've spoken to other MPs and local councillors and they take the same view. It simply would not be helpful." (It is worth nothing that, at a meeting at the House of Commons, in February 2001, organized by the *News of the World* in support of "Sarah's Law", a majority of the twenty or so MPs present took the same view.) However, some of those whom Syd Rapson represents disagree strongly.

Julie Waldram: "I think the *News of the World* did a brilliant job with the naming and shaming. I only wish they had carried it on. I support 'Sarah's Law' 110 per cent."

Sharon Mills: "I agree wholeheartedly with 'Sarah's Law'. This community [the c-word again] is already safer because of the action we took. But if the *News of the World* won the battle, it would make lots of other places safer from predatory paedophiles."

135

But those expecting Katrina Kessell to add her endorsement of community disclosure are in for a surprise. "People here don't want a 'Sarah's Law' because it's like naming and shaming. As soon as you name names, things kick off again and there's violence. As for the *News of the World*, well, they cocked up on a number of the names. What we want is for existing laws to be enforced, not new ones. Things like community protection orders. I tell you, the police just don't have a clue."

The priest, Father Gary Waddington, explains the profound differences in view like this: "A lot of people who protested were not representative of the community. They were what you might call the 'alienated within'. This was their way of making their presence felt."

So when it comes to supporting "Sarah's Law", which, according to the *News of the World*, attracted a million names to a petition delivered to the government, the "community" with supposedly the greatest interest in seeing it on the statute book is hopelessly split. Furthermore, what happened at Paulsgrove is a salutary reminder of how naming and shaming – far from boosting protection – almost inevitably turns people against one another and leads not only to violence but to a tide of suspicion and fear as well.

On one night alone, Syd Rapson had to arrange the rehousing of four families who had been targeted – with apparently little or no evidence to support the allegations against them. Two had the misfortune to have the same name as paedophiles living on the estate. The MP calls it the application of "summary justice". Though if he had chosen yet another historical parallel to reinforce his point, no one could blame him, because the affair reeks of the daily denunciations which characterized Soviet society during the Stalin Terror.

For example, Katrina Kessell made much of a list of suspected paedophiles which had been drawn up from "word of mouth and facts gleaned from the Internet". The protesters were convinced of the accuracy of the information they were using. Others said it was just the product of a rumour mill working overtime. Despite repeated entreaties to forward the list to the council, or at least allow it to be independently scrutinized, the protesters refused to make it public. Some senior police officers doubted that the list even existed and believed that it was being used to create fear and force certain people off the estate.

Even more disturbing is the claim that the list, real or imaginary, was merely a pretext for settling old scores – most of which had nothing to do with child sex abuse. The firebombing of the house next door to Syd Rapson and the torching of his neighbour's car while he was on holiday in Tenerife seems to fall into that category. Father Waddington formed the opinion that another agenda was playing alongside the paedophile one: "If there was a list – and I certainly didn't see it – there's a strong suspicion that the names were on it either because they had fallen foul of somebody or because they were regarded as a bit odd, a bit eccentric in some way. In other words, they were seen as soft targets."

With revenge masquerading as public concern, it is almost certain that, had the protests at Paulsgrove not ended when they did, even more trouble would have followed. Father Waddington, for one, is willing to speculate on the consequences if they had continued: "Over three or four days, I spoke to between 100 and 200 people on this estate and the consensus was that the protests were completely mad. And, in fact, if they had gone on, I believe we would have seen counter-protests and there could well have been a pitched battle."

Nappy Valley

As we have demonstrated, the events at Paulsgrove in August 2000 were the reaction of a working-class estate to a mixed bag of grievances. As a crude exercise in vigilantism, it had strengths and weaknesses. By pressing all the "right" buttons in this media age – children in push chairs, voluble and self-confident spokespeople, plus a dose of obligatory violence – it got instant attention, national and international. But because the emotion was raw and ugly and occasionally misdirected, it also attracted the almost universal censure of politicians, pundits and opinion-formers, to the point where, for several weeks, the thrust of articles in the press was not about the threat posed by paedophiles but about the unreasoning prejudice displayed by the ring-leaders.

Contrast this with the media coverage of another anti-paedophile protest which took place a few months after Paulsgrove and in a very different setting. In *The Times*, from 18 January, 2001, a long and detailed article begins like this: "What would you do if a paedophile moved next door? In Paulsgrove, they rioted. In Tooting, Lady Cosima Somerset and her neighbours are holding candlelit vigils."

If the dominant image of Paulsgrove was an unruly posse chanting "Sex crime, sex crime, hang them, hang them", that of Tooting was of well-scrubbed children holding balloons inscribed "Protect us please." Newspaper reports approvingly pointed out that the rudest placard here was one which read "Bog Off Boateng" [a reference to the Home Office minister responsible for sex offender issues at the time, Paul Boateng].

Just as the particular social geography of Paulsgrove helped shape the protests there, the same is true of the area of south London which the press dubbed "Nappy Valley", because so many young children live in the immediate vicinity. If the violence at Paulsgrove was largely the response of the alienated working class to having someone else's "problem" dumped on them, the protesters of Tooting tiptoed into the limelight like a reluctant guest at a sherry party. Having said that, the sense of grievance which impelled them to act was every bit as sharp as that felt by the protesters on the south coast. And every bit as successful. Just as the Paulsgrove action led to paedophiles being removed from the estate, so the middle-class women of Tooting managed to frustrate proposals to place a group of serious convicted offenders among them.

The problem began when it emerged that plans were quite far advanced to reopen a former bail and probation hostel for up to a dozen offenders deemed dangerous by the Home Office, some of whom would be paedophiles. The Victorian-era building is on Bedford Hill, which connects Balham to Streatham and runs across Tooting Common. The hostel had been used since the late 1970s, either for those considered in need of a halfway house to help them re-enter the community or for low-risk inmates subject to temporary bail conditions. Its presence had never excited any discernible interest or protest. When one of the authors went to visit a hostel resident in 1991, and asked someone living in the same road for directions, she had no idea where it was. This then is not an area where people live in each other's pockets. On the Heaver Estate – named after the nineteenth-century land developer Alfred Heaver – some of the four-bedroomed properties sell for £1 million. On the common, brisk Barbour-clad ladies in headscarves walk their dogs, and the early morning school run – there are prep schools nearby and nurseries with twee names like Teddies and Caterpillar – is likely to be by Range Rover. It would be a gross oversimplification to say that Tooting is all lawyers, bank managers and City traders, but there is a strong feel, as in neighbouring Wandsworth and

Battersea, of people living self-reliant lives with an inbuilt suspicion of big government.

As it happens, the brand of government in 2000 has a relevance to the protests. Not for the obvious reason that it was New Labour and many of the protesters might be considered natural Tories. In fact, like hundreds of thousands of others across the country, deep disillusion with the fag-end of eighteen years of Conservative rule had prompted many in this part of south London to switch allegiance in 1997 and vote in Tony Blair.

But Wandsworth Borough Council, once the local government flagship of Thatcherism, was still Conservative controlled. And as Christmas 2000 approached, someone working for the council – reportedly a housing officer – contacted the local newspaper, the *Wandsworth Guardian*, with a juicy story. Backed up by minutes of a crucial meeting, the news was that the Home Office and an organization which it funded, the Langley House Trust, were in discussions about reopening the Bedford Hill hostel, which had been closed for about a year. And what got the newsdesk salivating was the revelation that, this time, the residents would be high-risk offenders, among them "dangerous" paedophiles.

The plan was to house twelve convicted offenders at the hostel, all of whom had volunteered for treatment after completing their sentence. In the words of the Trust, they were people "who had carried out robberies using extreme violence or committed sexual abuse against children or committed minor theft but had some violent fantasy." In the post-Paulsgrove climate, it was evident that these were people who would be difficult to place anywhere in the country without provoking an almighty row once the intention became public. But Bedford Hill presented one enormous advantage. Since planning permission already existed for the hostel, a lot of the difficulties over change of use could be side-stepped.

So, during November 2000, the scheme was finalized at meetings between the Langley House Trust, the Inner London probation service, Wandsworth social services, housing and other agencies. All under the watchful gaze of the Home Office – but, crucially, without the knowledge of local residents. Then, when the *Wandsworth Guardian* hit the streets in early December, the storm broke.

Gina Birley lives in Old Devonshire Road, a brisk ten-minute walk from the Bedford Hill hostel. She's a teacher and school governor, and has two teenage children and a strong sense of civic responsibility. She was not in the vanguard of the protest and, indeed, at first, had strong doubts about taking to the streets at all: "Frankly, it was Paulsgrove which made me hesitate. I dislike any kind of mob rule or violence and I found the scenes from Paulsgrove shown on television very frightening indeed. And though the people here are rather more articulate, I was concerned that something similar might erupt in Tooting."

Concerned she might well have been, because Gina Birley knows something about the law. She's a magistrate. "I was familiar with the building in Bedford Hill. I used to send people there in my capacity on the bench. But they were offenders at the less dangerous end of the spectrum. Not high-risk paedophiles."

What persuaded her to overcome her initial reluctance was not so much what was being proposed as the way it was being done. And here, despite the demographic differences from Paulsgrove, we can see some of the same forces at play – especially the perceived cynicism of the authorities responsible for housing sex offenders:

> The Langley House Trust and the Inner London probation service got everybody's backs up. They proposed the first public meeting for thirteen days *after* the hostel was due to reopen. They made it absolutely clear that this scheme was not open to negotiation. It was coming. Period.
>
> But they also tried to mislead. Initially, they said it would not be for serious offenders. Then they started dropping terms like *public protection orders*. Well, to anybody in the know, that gave the game away. Piecing together the picture, it was obvious that the Home Office had, for some time, been looking at places to open such a hostel on an experimental basis, and when they checked the register of properties, they must have thought: 'Hey, we've got a site in Wandsworth and we don't need permission because it's already got it. Let's get the ball rolling.'

Anyone who expects the Home Office – whatever the persuasion of government in power – to admit to such a charge would be breathtakingly naïve. Civil-service policy-making is invariably wrapped up in serpentine complexities, one of the purposes of which is to hide the truth from the prying gaze of the media. So, on this occasion, we are grateful to officials from the Dangerous Offenders Unit for helping to signpost the future direction of policy on siting of hostels for released paedophiles and, in so doing, tacitly conceding that consultation with local communities has tended to be on the margin of the agenda for police, probation services, councils and other agencies.

One senior civil servant put it like this. "We hope that the new duties on these agencies under the Criminal Justice and Court Services Act 2000 will make them far more proactive in discussing the risks with communities and getting an informal debate going with them. We are working on a new strategy for hostels to get an even demographic spread of the burden across the country – and to remind people that the inmates of these hostels often come from the same communities as them and are not aliens."

The point about an even spread of the burden is particularly relevant to Wandsworth. *Gina Birley*:

> You know, in this council ward alone, there are thirty-six supported housing schemes. One road, Byrne Road, has three or four. Of course, not all are for released offenders, but anyone can see that there are a lot of vulnerable people in this borough.
>
> Now this raises two issues. To put dangerous paedophiles into an area could have unforeseen consequences for some of the mentally ill and homeless in these schemes by making the whole environment here more volatile. So it's not just the community at risk, but people within the community who deserve special protection and are being denied it.
>
> Also, it stands to reason that if you put a hostel for paedophiles somewhere, it has to be with the consent of the community, because you can't rehabilitate them into the community – which presumably is the aim – if you infuriate people by not telling them in the first place that the paedophiles are going to be placed there.

Taking a step back from the partisanship of the fray, such arguments could be seen as a classic NIMBY ("not in my back yard") stance: yes, by all means try to integrate paedophiles back into the community – as long as it is not ours. The aggrieved managers of the Langley House Trust certainly level that criticism. The chief executive of the trust, John Adams, argues that he and his colleagues were dealing with some closed minds when they sought to put their case to the representatives of the "community", though he is also candid about mistakes made on his side:

> There was a meeting with local councillors on 5 December, 2000, and it did not go well. They were there not to listen but to express their anger and opposition. Most of their ammunition came from notes, far from accurate, taken by a housing officer at a meeting of professionals where we thought we were among colleagues. That was

when the first headline appeared, saying that a paedophile hostel was planned. Together with press officers from the police and probation service, we produced a nondescript press release, a holding operation to see how things developed. It was not going to convince anybody and, with hindsight, we should have had a proactive campaign in place before we even set foot in the territory. We had done our preparations on inter-agency social work and risk management, but there was nothing on the PR side.

He points out that there was a lack of information in the public domain about the work of hostels and the sort of treatment programmes available. Indeed, the substitute for hard fact was probation service jargon – like the approach known as "What Works" – which wouldn't begin to impress the sceptical layman: "'What Works' is professional-speak, and the public is still firmly of the view that nothing works when it comes to rehabilitating offenders. In the area around the hostel, fear was easily generated. We were unable to provide statistics in support of arguments that hostels reduce crime and do not have a negative impact on the immediate neighbourhood."

It is highly improbable that, even if such arguments had been backed up by solid evidence, they would have made much headway in the area around Bedford Hill. Such was the fury over the way that news of the scheme had broken. Contemporary newspaper interviews with residents are littered with such words as "shocking" and "underhand" to describe the perceived lack of consultation.

Gina Birley links this with a more general feeling of disillusionment with government, local and national. "I think a lot more people feel disenfranchised than three or four years ago, that democratic means of protest are being denied to them. And because their elected representatives are not listening, you have moderate people being driven to immoderate action. In my field, criminal justice, there's a growing view that the rights of the accused are more important than those of the victim. I think all these things were behind the action taken here."

In one sense, this is a case of "so far, so predictable". To some, it may sound like the kind of saloon-bar diatribe which bemoaned the murder conviction in 1999 of the Norfolk farmer Tony Martin for shooting a teenage burglar on his property. Or the fury of the fuel protesters who blocked Britain's main roads and caused temporary panic during the autumn of 2000. If you like, the dispossessed – or self-styled dispossessed – flexing their muscles.

Such manifestations of anger invariably attract those with other, more overtly party-political, agendas. At Paulsgrove, the British

National Party tried to capitalize on the protests. The MP, Syd Rapson, was sent anti-paedophile material through the post which he recognized as coming from a BNP source. And the Tooting protesters were warned that the BNP might try to infiltrate a march or come to meetings. In the event, it didn't happen (street protests in a bitterly cold January and February don't have the same appeal as those in the long, light nights of August). But Gina Birley and some of the campaigners became alarmed at the company they were keeping:

> It wasn't until about the fourth committee meeting that I realized that there were some serious fascists involved. Some of the views expressed were unprintable – you know, "why don't we just cut their bits off", that kind of thing. A few people were against hostels altogether, which didn't reflect my view at all. Then there were the local Tories who wanted to exploit the publicity by claiming that it was a Tory-controlled council which had leaked the plans. I think it was at that point that I and a few others became rather uncomfortable with the way things were going.

So once again, as with Paulsgrove, the *News of the World* notion that here was a homogeneous community which needed to be defended and protected breaks down. If anything, the pressure of the protests helped emphasize splits and differences among the campaigners rather than bringing them together.

Gina Birley: "We discussed community disclosure and I am against it. First of all, what would you do with the information that a paedophile was living in your road? I might use it responsibly but many people would not. Secondly, why community disclosure only for paedophiles? Why don't banks write to their customers to tell them that a convicted bank robber has moved into the neighbourhood? There's simply no logic to it."

And even allowing for the fact that protection of our children will always, quite rightly, assume greater importance than safeguarding the vaults of the local bank, it has to be said that she is right. There's simply no logic to it.

Conclusion

We have pointed out the contrasting social contexts to the protests at Paulsgrove and Tooting and drawn attention to what they had in common. It will be noted that the most influential common denominator is the perception in both communities that they were being treated unfairly, and that decisions about placing released paedophiles were being taken without due consultation.

Leaving aside the merits, or otherwise, of the protests, there is little doubt that this perception reflects reality, that, in the equation of policy-making, the one factor which has been consistently overlooked has been the local population. Almost exactly a year after the anti-Bedford Hill campaign, another commuter-belt community took to the streets to protest about paedophiles – this time at Chertsey in Surrey. We will discuss this in more detail in the next chapter on the role of the media, but it is worth noting at this stage that the reason for intervening given by Beverley Hughes, Paul Boateng's successor at the Home Office, was her belief that the necessary consultation procedures had not been fulfilled.

And if one looks at the bigger picture, that is to say, government strategy on sex offenders over the last twenty years, it is hardly surprising that these flaws have been inflicting damage. Until the late 1980s, no one at the Home Office had given any serious thought as to what should be done with sex offenders other than locking them up and, if necessary, segregating them for their own protection under what was then called Rule 43.

Then it was accepted that treatment, in the form of cognitive therapy, should be administered. So began the prison service Sex Offender Treatment Programme. It was not until 1997 and the Sex Offender Act that any serious thought was given to how to manage the risks to the public posed by paedophiles. As we outline in chapter 1, this act created the Sex Offender Register, which, despite dominating the debate about the public's "right to know", promised more than it could deliver by way of community protection. Moreover, it was a continuation of the top-down approach which has signally failed to give due weight to local concerns. Only with the Criminal Justice and Court Services Act 2000 and the creation of the Multi-Agency Public Protection Panels (MAPPPs) was a new phase of localized community involvement launched.

Even so, no one is yet talking about the kind of public meetings which are routinely called in some states in America to inform people about the release of dangerous paedophiles into their area (Washington state is a notable example). One official at the National Probation Directorate, who has spent time in Seattle, told the authors that Britain was "not ready" for such grassroots involvement.

Ironically, it seems that the United States – the home of red-necked vigilantism – is able to handle this kind of information more responsibly than the UK. There may be a number of reasons for that, but one is undoubtedly the role played by the media. And that is what we consider next.

8

Named and Shamed

There is one form of human life lower than a paedophile and that is the editor of a national newspaper who uses the parents of a murdered child, while they are still in shock, to bolster circulation figures.

Letter to The Guardian, *8 August 2001*

Introduction

If you bought a copy of the *News of the World* on any Sunday between the end of July 2000 and Christmas 2001, you would probably have noticed, just below the masthead, the words "For Sarah". It was a reference to Sarah Payne, the eight-year-old Sussex girl whose murder at the beginning of July 2000 prompted the newspaper to launch a campaign of naming and shaming paedophiles, the repercussions of which dominated news coverage for many weeks. The paper's editor, Rebekah Wade, promised that "For Sarah" would appear on every edition until the government brought in legislation which gave people the right to know if a convicted sex offender was living in their area.

It is a long – and sometimes honourable – tradition that newspapers do not merely report the news, they make it. William Randolph Hearst, the model for the film *Citizen Kane*, understood the power of the press and wielded it like a broadsword. In Britain, the rival barons Beaverbrook and Northcliffe used the *Daily Express* and *Daily Mail* respectively as much to propagandize as to disseminate news. So when, on 23 July 2000, the *News of the World* carried a picture of Sarah Payne on its front page next to a pledge to name and shame every one of 110,000 convicted child sex offenders in the UK, it could be argued that it was merely following in the buccaneering footsteps of some of its predecessors.

But this was campaigning journalism without a parallel in this country. The *News of the World* was not merely lobbying for a change in the law, it was using an entire group of people – convicted paedophiles – as live bait. It was, in effect, issuing a challenge to its four million readers. It was saying to them: "these people, the lowest of the low, are an active and ongoing threat to your children. What are you going to do about it?"

We have already recorded what some of them did at Paulsgrove. In this chapter, we interpret the challenge in a rather more responsible way, by examining the consequences of a "Sarah's Law" for public protection and asking whether some sections of the media can continue to play the role of *agent provocateur* without being held accountable for the damage done. We hear from the police and probation service, from a former home secretary and from a convicted paedophile – and we attempt to talk to the managing editor of the *News of the World*. That encounter did not turn out as planned, but it does provide some powerful and illuminating insights into what one might call the Wapping Mindset.

All the news that's fit to print

Journalistic memories are notoriously short, and the furore which followed that first naming and shaming edition of the *News of the World* on 23 July had a distinctly "Year Zero" tinge to it – in other words, nothing which had gone before could compare with the new and terrible landscape which had been opened up. But that was not so. It is true that the way in which *News of the World* executives justified their campaign took the self-serving arrogance of some parts of the press to new heights, but on the substance – the identification of paedophiles through photographs and addresses published in a newspaper, sometimes with horrendous consequences – we had been here before.

For example, in February 1997, Francis Duffy, a man of sixty-seven suffering from senile dementia, was battered and kicked by a mob of local people in Manchester near the hostel where he lived. For good measure they poured blue paint over him as well. The attackers believed, following the publication of a picture in the *Manchester Evening News*, that Mr Duffy was a convicted paedophile. Unfortunately (for the victim) the picture was of another man, Brynley Dummett, who had six convictions for child sex offences. Mr Dummett had been living on a housing estate at Ancoats, and the editor of the *Manchester Evening News*, Mike Unger, defended his decision to publish on the grounds that Dummett was befriending children close to his flat.

The fiasco was compounded when, following the assault on the wrong man, Dummett fled from his home and the police admitted they had lost track of him.

Mike Unger reportedly accepted no responsibility for the incident and said the publication reflected the public's concern. He wasn't alone in his thinking. Around the same time, the *Evening Mail* in Birmingham was also running a campaign to "out" local paedophiles. And in Reading, a convicted burglar who was wearing an electronic tag was attacked by a gang after a newspaper ran a story that a sex offender in the town was subject to electronic monitoring.

These incidents flickered briefly in the local and regional media but made little national impact. However, in 1998, the release from prison of one of the country's most notorious paedophile killers, Sidney Cooke, raised the stakes and placed the issue of vigilantism on every front page and TV news bulletin.

Cooke, part of the gang (including Robert Oliver and Lennie Smith) who had killed fourteen-year-old Jason Swift during a sex orgy in 1985, was held at a police station in the West Country while discussions went on about his longer-term future. Violent demonstrations, in which bricks and petrol bombs were thrown, took place outside police stations in Bristol, Yeovil, Minehead and Bridgewater. The police believed that at least one of the protests was caused by a story in a local newspaper that a man with a blanket over his head had been taken into a station in Knowle West. As with the Manchester incident, the facts were wrong. In this case, the story was based on a hoax call. It prompted the Yeovil MP, Paddy Ashdown – then leader of the Liberal Democrats – to issue a statement on 23 April 1998 which said, in part: "Unfortunately some local press coverage has been irresponsible and exploitative. Local newspapers have a duty to their communities – they should inform not inflame."

These are just a few episodic examples of media-related violence, but more extensive evidence was collected by the Association of

Chief Officers of Probation which found that, in the year preceding the release of Sidney Cooke, there had been more than forty such incidents around the country. And when the *News of the World* embarked on its supposedly ground-breaking naming and shaming enterprise in the summer of 2000, it was already a recidivist in this field. In 1996, it had been responsible for driving a released paedophile, Jimmy Larwood, from his home in south-east London. After his council flat had been broken into and wrecked, a *News of the World* article describing him as a "sex pervert" was found pinned to a wall.

News values

There are certain crimes which have a resonance that seems to grow, rather than, as one might expect, diminish, with the passing of time. Frequently, they involve children – usually as victims but sometimes as perpetrators. The Moors Murders are one obvious example, with the question of any possible release for Myra Hindley even more emotive now than at any time over the past three decades. The same is true of the killing of two-year-old James Bulger in 1993. The release of his murderers, Robert Thompson and Jon Venables, in the summer of 2001 raised many of the fears about vigilantism which we have seen in paedophile cases.

The murder of eight-year-old Sarah Payne in July 2000 is notable not so much for the crime itself – horrible though it was – but for the chord it struck in the media. It is not hard to see why. One minute Sarah was playing with her three siblings in a cornfield near her grandparents' home near Littlehampton in Sussex, and the next she had disappeared without trace. The subsequent hunt was one of the largest ever mounted by a police force and ended sixteen days later when her body was found by a labourer in a shallow grave in a field about 12 miles away, near Pulborough.

The bald facts alone made it a potent "story". But two other elements gave it the kind of staying power which made the *News of the World*'s naming and shaming campaign almost a seamless extension of the reporting of the crime. One was the deliberate decision of the police to encourage media interest in the hope of teasing out vital clues to a disappearance which – on the face of it – was baffling. Daily on-camera press briefings at the police incident room were designed to keep media attention focused on Sussex rather than straying to events elsewhere. Indeed, a senior officer candidly admitted that he dreaded the moment when the TV satellite trucks moved on. The other factor was the extraordinarily high profile adopted by Sarah's parents, Sara and Michael – especially Sara, confident and telegenic, who was rarely off the television screens over those sixteen days. She – and the constantly shown photos of her blonde, wide-eyed daughter in her gingham shirt – gave this crime a human face, and it is difficult to ignore a human face in acute distress.

But the news media is not driven by sentiment, and in the ferociously competitive world of the tabloid press decisions about coverage are invariably made with circulation and readership profile in mind. In the 1990s, crime and "law and order" had been exploited by newspaper executives time and again to force up sales, one example being the conviction for murder in 1999 of the Norfolk farmer Tony Martin, who shot a teenaged burglar who had entered his home. With its brilliantly honed instinct for "Middle England" populism, the *Daily Mail* was the first national paper to grasp the sense of outrage it could tap among its readers, and it launched a campaign on behalf of the farmer.

In 1999, the present editor of the *News of the World*, Rebekah Wade, was deputy editor of *The Sun* and, reportedly, had also wanted her newspaper to endorse Tony Martin's case; but she failed to convince her bosses. It seems that she remembered the lesson from *The Mail*, though, and waited for the next opportunity to put it to profitable use. After Sarah Payne's murder, the *News of the World* commissioned some market research and found that a strong campaign on the issue of paedophiles would play well among its four million readers. It was launched on 23 July 2000.

Unanswered questions

Rebekah Wade rarely gives interviews to other journalists. Whether this is because of shyness or haughtiness or plain contrariness, it's hard to say. And as the maelstrom of criticism (and, to be fair, a measure of support) swirled around her in July 2000, she was characteristically unavailable to defend her stance. When the authors asked for a chance to put questions, they were told by the *News of the World's* PR manager, Hayley Barlow, that they could speak to the managing editor, Stuart Kuttner, instead. The following is an account (written immediately afterwards so it is not a verbatim transcript – for reasons which will become clear) of what happened when the offer was taken up in his glass-fronted office at the paper's Wapping headquarters.

The letter "K" represents Kuttner and "A" is for author. Strangely, you might think, the first question was put by Mr Kuttner:

K: Have you come to interview me?
A: (somewhat surprised): Yes.
K: Oh, I thought this was just a preliminary chat.
A: No, I made a formal request for an interview and it was agreed and arranged for today.

There was then a brief silence while the author produced a mini-disc from his shoulder bag with which he intended to record the conversation to supplement shorthand notes. This provoked a frisson of concern in Mr Kuttner.

K: I'd rather you didn't set that up until we've talked this through. To begin with, what is your stance on our naming and shaming campaign? What line are you planning to take in the book?

At this early point it would have been perfectly possible to dissemble, to say something to please and placate the interviewee even if it was some way from the truth. After all, isn't that the staple approach of the doorstep hack desperate to persuade a reluctant "victim" to talk for a splash story? But, apart from the ethical problem of lying – no small consideration, it must be said – it hardly seemed necessary between two mature journalists on a matter which had been in the public domain for many months. Thus, the author, adopting honesty as the best, indeed only, policy, explained that he had serious misgivings about the campaign while remaining neutral about the need for a so-called Sarah's Law. This answer did not please Mr Kuttner:

K: Why should we cooperate with a book when it is clearly going to be critical of the *News of the World*?
A: Well, if you believe in democracy and a free press – which I assume you do – then a pluralism of views is an essential part of that process. Surely, what matters is whether I report your views faithfully – and I will.

151

K: All of our views are already in the public domain. We're happy to give you everything we have said, which is in the public domain.

The encounter seemed to be getting more surreal by the moment. Here was a busy newspaper executive who, at the outset, had said that his time was limited, filibustering like a diehard MP desperate to kill an unwelcome bill. At this point, seeking to steer the conversation on to less emotive ground, it was suggested to him that the question of how to deal with paedophiles – perhaps more than any other offenders – needed a cool and objective head.

K: No. Talk to Sara and Michael Payne. Talk to the parents of other murdered children. Then tell me you want to be cool and objective. On the contrary, you should be emotive about this.
A: Perhaps there's not a lot to be gained in talking about our approach. What's important is that we share the same objective – which is child protection.
K: I don't know whether we do.

From then on, including some pointless questions about whether the author had children, we continued deeper into the cul-de-sac. The non-interview interview had taken at least fifty minutes and ended with an assurance by Mr Kuttner that he would consider whether he should grant a "proper" interview at a later date. Needless to say, it did not happen, and there was no further direct contact with the *News of the World* (although we shall return, via a different route, to the paper's defence of its campaign).

The conclusions which may be drawn from this experience are a matter for the reader. Anyone who has got this far will be in no doubt about the authors' standpoint, but it is time to introduce some other interested parties who were scorched by the bushfire lit by the *News of the World*'s naming and shaming campaign.

Damage limitation

The two organizations with the principal statutory responsibility for protecting the public from dangerous offenders are the police and the probation service. Their representative bodies are, respectively, the Association of Chief Police Officers (ACPO) and the Association of Chief Officers of Probation (ACOP). In 2000, by a curious coincidence, the spokespersons on sex offender issues for the two associations both worked in Gloucestershire. Gill Mackenzie (quoted in chapter 7) was the county's chief probation officer and Tony Butler its chief constable. They had worked closely together for a number of years and forged a bond based on common principles. That unity was put to a severe test by the naming and shaming campaign and its consequences.

Gill Mackenzie: "It may sound a bit strong to compare the uproar and damage caused by the *News of the World* to the events associated with Fascism in Italy and Germany before the war, but that's what it seemed like. The focusing of hatred on one group in the community; the manipulation of the mob; the pain and suffering inflicted on innocent people – and I don't mean paedophiles but people mistaken for paedophiles or the children of families who were attacked in their homes. And of course, it gave a licence to all sorts of violent behaviour. For example, a number of the assaults were racially motivated and nothing to do with paedophilia. Yes, the *News of the World* was highlighting a serious issue, but it did it in a violent and unyielding way which did far more harm than good."

Tony Butler: "The *News of the World* helped devalue the word 'paedophile' to the point where it just causes confusion. If you put ten people in a room, you would get ten different definitions of what a paedophile is. The biggest danger is what I call the 'serial boyfriend' who moves in and out of families, often targeting the pre-teenage daughter (and, sometimes, the son). He knows damn well that, if the child reports the abuse, they may well end up losing the mother as well, so the abuser has a powerful hold over the victim. Now, how does that kind of person equate to the predatory offender like Robert Oliver or Sydney Cooke? Is there any point in labelling them both 'paedophiles'?"

Butler and Mackenzie were at the eye of the storm in the summer of 2000. For a fortnight, they struggled to cope with the outbreaks of disorder which followed the first issue of the *News of the World* to name and shame paedophiles, while at the same time trying to negotiate a way out of the crisis with Rebekah Wade and Stuart Kuttner. In the background – when it should have been firmly in the foreground – was the Home Office, caught in its own dilemma of how to stick to its policy on sex offenders without alienating the Murdoch press, which New Labour had courted assiduously since before the 1997 election. It was a potent mix of interests.

Gill Mackenzie picked up on one aspect of this symbiotic relationship between ministers and media early on: "There were times
during meetings when Rebekah Wade talked of the home secretary
as though he was a puppet whom she could manipulate. In fact,
there was something frighteningly contemptuous of politicians and
democracy as a whole in the *News of the World*'s attitude."

But, if News International's behaviour was true to form, so was
that of the government. During the protests over the released child
killer Sydney Cooke in 1998, ministers were conspicuous by their
absence from the public debate which filled the newspaper columns
and airwaves for days on end. And the same applies to the events of
August 2000. Indeed, at the height of the controversy, Tony Butler
sent a letter to the "duty" Home Office minister and did not even
get a reply. However, when it came to responding to communica-
tions from the *News of the World*, all speed was the watchword.

For example, on 13 September 2000, Rebekah Wade sent a letter to the home secretary, Jack Straw, explaining that his plans to
strengthen the arrangements for protecting the public from sex
offenders did not go far enough. (Her letter also misrepresents
Tony Butler's views on controlled access to information on sex
offenders – but that is by the by.) That same evening, at 8.30 p.m.,
an official in the Home Office's Mental Health Unit sent out a draft
of Mr Straw's reply to interested parties as an email attachment, and
invited comments. The official explained that "the Home Secretary
will need to reply to Rebekah Wade tomorrow so, with apologies
for yet another unreasonable deadline, could I ask for comments by
11.30 tomorrow please."

That email is one of a number of documents we have obtained
during the course of research for this book which cast a revealing
light on the inner working of government when faced with a "crisis".
They show, for example, that the Home Office considered taking
out an injunction to prevent the *News of the World* continuing its
naming and shaming campaign. The first ground to be explored was
the use of confidential information on paedophiles obtained from
the Scout Association. The association had a comprehensive archive
on convicted sex offenders going back a number of years, and many
of the names included in the 23 July edition of the *News of the
World* appear to have been culled from these files.

An email from a senior official in the Mental Health Unit, sent on
28 July, makes it plain that this course was rejected for two reasons.
First, because some of the names held by the Scout Association had

been taken from local newspapers and were therefore already in the public domain. And second, because ministers were afraid that the *News of the World* would present this as "an assault on press freedom". Indeed, the messages flying back and forth at the Home Office make it plain that it was this second issue, the political dimensions of the problem, which was causing by far the greatest concern.

On 27 July, an official from the Home Office legal department wrote to the Mental Health Unit, setting out his views on the difficulties: "To stand any chance of success [of securing an injunction] we would need concrete evidence that the work of the probation service was being impeded by the publications and that sex offenders were going underground and breaching their licence conditions. It would be important to show that this was creating a serious risk to the public from the offenders themselves. ... It would also be important to show that the sex offenders were themselves at risk from assaults etc."

As we shall see, this "concrete evidence" was not only available, it was collated by ACPO and ACOP in a joint dossier presented to the Press Complaints Commission on 17 August 2000. But other passages from the email show that the wider political considerations overrode all others:

> The prospect of the Home Secretary obtaining an injunction to prevent the *News of the World* publishing photographs and information about sex offenders in the community seems pretty remote to me and will cause an enormous outcry about attempts to "gag the press". So, there are huge political dimensions to this and I have no doubt that authority to proceed with any such application would have to come not just from the Home Secretary but probably from No 10 too . . . Can I summarise by saying "yes", it may be possible, but taking on Fleet Street is no small matter in political terms and previous governments have often come to grief in the process.

As experienced government-watchers, we have often observed that, whereas for ministers – especially at the Home Office – the instinct is to do something, even if it is the wrong thing, their civil servants have a genetic predisposition for masterly inaction. On this occasion, the civil servants carried the day and were proved right. On 28 July, an official in the Mental Health Unit set out the Home Office strategy. It was "to keep up the pressure on the *News of the World* to help get themselves off the hook once they are brought to the point of wanting to. The *News of the World* has committed the cardinal military error of entering the battle without securing its line of retreat, so we need to help it to do that."

That point was reached more quickly than he might have anticipated. On 2 August, after two editions of the *News of the World* in which paedophiles were named and shamed, Rebekah Wade announced the suspension (in reality the abandoning) of the campaign. It would be fascinating to know what she now thinks of the Home Office battle plan to get her to do that, and whether she is prepared to acknowledge that it had any effect on her decision. But we are not holding our breath for any confession about that aspect of the story!

Rebekah Wade was determined that her announcement should have the collective endorsement of the other key parties – ACOP and ACPO. This was highly inconvenient for Tony Butler, who was at home in rural Gloucestershire: "I knew there was no way I could get to London in time for the press conference, but Rebekah insisted that I had to be there, so a News International helicopter was dispatched to fetch me. I was amazed, given that our force helicopter cost £800 an hour to run and in eight years as chief constable I had never once found a justification for using it for personal transport. There's the power of the press for you."

Of course, what lay behind all the news conferences, the negotiations and strategic thinking was an ugly situation threatening to become even uglier every day. All over the country, probation and police officers involved in child protection were being distracted from their job in order to prevent sex offenders abandoning treatment courses and, in some cases, fleeing their homes. As we mentioned, a dossier of incidents was presented to the Press Complaints Commission by ACPO and ACOP to substantiate their case that the *News of the World* had behaved irresponsibly. It collated data under three categories – the same categories as the Home Office lawyer, quoted above, had identified as being necessary to justify applying for an injunction. We quote from the dossier:

1   *The campaign put children at risk by reducing the compliance of those sex offenders in contact with statutory services with child protection duties.* ACOP has case-study evidence that shows the common reaction of sex offenders under supervision following publication was to consider moving away from their home area and to change their name and appearance – effectively going underground and removing themselves from police and probation monitoring. In these

circumstances, the risk to children increases. Reports show that several offenders did abscond.

Probation, with the police, have had to make contingency arrangements to move sex offenders who were identified by the *News of the World* or were "outed" locally. This often disrupts settled patterns of supervision and monitoring, including covert surveillance on the part of the police.

The isolation, depression and feelings of persecution felt by offenders by the threat of publicity – although they might warrant little sympathy – are often trigger factors in offending behaviour. Risk management is made more difficult.

2   *The campaign caused distress to innocent third parties.* Although all the information printed had at one time been in the public domain, the campaign did not consider the impact on innocent members of sex offenders' families who were being "shamed" by association. Fear of publication was widespread. Victims, who might be trying to put their trauma behind them, also reasonably feared identification. The fact that many victims are also relatives of their offender doubles the potential for distress.

3   *The campaign created a permissive climate for extreme intolerance and incited (often random) violence.* Reports of vigilante action that has spilled over into public disorder are well documented in the press and media reports. Beneath this, there are a considerable number of unreported incidents of assault and threats. Also local leafleting, based on "name and shame", have sprung up. Most use dubious information and many are explicitly threatening. All heighten fear in every section of the community.

Tony Butler saw a number of examples in his own county to back up the dossier:

> The tension caused by naming and shaming was extremely damaging for the long-term personal relationships which we and the probation service had built up with released paedophiles. Some believed the police had leaked information to the *News of the World* , so that vital element of trust was broken. An offender in Gloucestershire, who'd been convicted seventeen years earlier, phoned me one day to say he was desperately concerned not just for his own safety but for his family – his wife was having chemotherapy for cancer. In fact, he was so desperate that he fled to Scotland for a fortnight. He came back, but, even though we put an alarm on his house and provided surveillance, he wouldn't stay there and moved into lodgings.

157

Another sex offender in Gloucestershire, with one conviction more than six years earlier, wrote a long and extremely well-argued letter to his chief constable, explaining why he was moving to another part of the country. We quote from part of it:

> I have not reoffended – nor do I ever intend to. I have never hidden or changed my name. I work sixteen hours a week in a voluntary capacity for a national charity (I do NOT come into contact with any children whatsoever). It is untrue that all convicted sex offenders will reoffend. There are many, like myself, who have reformed and there are government statistics to prove it. I am not asking for sympathy but I might add that I was given a lengthy prison sentence. I am now sixty-one years of age, 85 per cent disabled, have a serious heart condition and diabetes. I lost my business, my home and my so-called friends turned their backs on me. Having paid my debt to society, what right does the *News of the World* have to punish me all over again? They act as judge and jury and under the guise of protecting the public, incite what can only be described as mob rule. . . . Please, please try to help me.
>
> [Signed] A desperate man at my wits end.

The paper speaks!

Had we interviewed the managing editor of the *News of the World*, we would have shown him that letter and asked for his response. As we have explained, that opportunity was denied to us. However, in November 2000 the paper's PR manager, Hayley Barlow, answered a series of questions put by Sonia Millington, a masters student in criminal justice policy at the University of Central England. For the sake of balance, we quote a section of it.

> Q: Were you aware of the potential dangers that the [naming and shaming] campaign could cause?
> A: Oh, yes, very much so.
> Q: Do you feel any responsibility for the vigilante attacks that occurred as a result of the campaign?
> A: We don't take any responsibility in the sense that, right from the word go, our core objective with this campaign was to warn, to alert but definitely not to incite. Unfortunately, in this country . . . there are a handful of people who see fit to take the law into their

own hands. All the attacks that took place, bar one [that one being Victor Burnett at Paulsgrove], were mistaken identities and people who we had not named and shamed in the newspaper . . .

Q: So you don't take any responsibility for the violence?

A: No.

Other views

One thing conspicuously absent from the *News of the World*'s campaign was any acknowledgement of the arguments against public access to information about released paedophiles. We do not mean the arguments from other newspaper columnists or, indeed, from aggrieved (and therefore, interested) parties such as the convicted offender who wrote to Tony Butler. But what about the powerful argument set out in a High Court judgment of July 1997 to which we referred briefly in chapter 1 (*R* v. *Chief Constable of North Wales Police*, ex p. AB and CD)? After all, this judgment – delivered by the then lord chief justice, Lord Bingham (sitting, unusually, in the divisional court), and later upheld by the Court of Appeal – represented the law of the land at the time of the *News of the World*'s naming and shaming campaign. And even if the paper disagreed with it, it was shabby journalism to ignore it.

The case involved a husband and wife, convicted sex offenders, who moved to a caravan site near Wrexham in 1996 following their release from long prison sentences. After receiving a report from another force describing the pair as "extremely dangerous people who would pose a considerable risk to children and vulnerable adults", North Wales Police (NWP) alerted the owner of the site to their presence. The pair sought judicial review of the police action on the grounds of unlawfulness.

Lord Bingham rejected their case but, in so doing, said the following: "Had the NWP operated a *blanket* policy of disclosure, it would have been legally objectionable. . . . a *general* policy of disclosure can never be justified, and the media should be slow to obstruct the rehabilitation of ex-offenders who have not offended again and who are seriously bent on reform." In upholding the judgment in March 1998, the Master of the Rolls, Lord Woolf (the present Lord Chief Justice), said disclosure should be made only when there was "a pressing need for it".

In one sense, the question of vigilantism and paedophiles being driven underground, though it garnered all the headlines during the naming and shaming episode, is not the real issue. What lies at the heart of this book is child protection and how to put in place measures which will achieve that goal. This is where the *News of the World* stands accused, at best, of naivety, and, at worst, of hypocrisy, because by its grotesque oversimplification of the problem – identifying all paedophiles as potentially dangerous predators – it actually put more children at risk. And if the newspaper had spent a fraction of the time that it devoted to thoughtless posturing analysing the psychology of paedophilia, it would have known that that was a likely consequence.

Gerald, the convicted paedophile whom we met in Chapter 3, was living in south London when the 23 July edition of the *News of the World* was published. Having battled for years with chronically low self-esteem, he had been feeling slightly more confident and was working again. Those links with the community which are crucial in suppressing a paedophile's desire to offend were beginning to be re-established. Then, suddenly, consternation:

> For that first week after July 23, I was scared and panicky. Logically, I knew that it could be years before the *News of the World* got round to naming and shaming me, but your mind doesn't work logically. I was worried about staying at home, so I kept going to places where I wasn't known. One day, I even took a coach up to Scotland. It was getting silly. It took a full week before I got the courage to pick up the phone to the clinic [the Wolvercote residential clinic in Epsom which treats adult sex offenders] and ask for help. By the time the second edition came out, I was back at Wolvercote, so I felt safer.

So far, perhaps, so predictable. But here's the really important admission:

> What the naming and shaming did was to push my self-esteem down to rock bottom. And that's when a paedophile is most likely to act on his fantasies. What the *News of the World* did was to get me back into an offending frame of mind. I thought, "well, if I'm going to be named and publicly humiliated, what's the point of trying to develop a life, because I'm not going to get the chance anyway." That set me thinking about children again and saying to myself, "well, they enjoyed it when I was with them, etc." Frankly, if I hadn't managed to get back into the clinic, I really think I would have abused another child.

And this is the psychology which the *News of the World* fails to understand by promoting its "Sarah's Law". The public access to information which it believes will make the community safer may well have exactly the opposite effect. Paedophiles like Gerald, who are striving for some kind of stake in society, no matter how tenuous, are far more likely to control their urge to offend (by recourse to *inhibitors*, as the psychological jargon has it) than those who feel vulnerable and at risk of exposure.

> Even before I was convicted, I didn't feel part of the community because, although nobody else knew what I was doing and what was going on in my mind, I did. And feeling outside the community is dangerous for me because it makes developing relations with adults even more difficult. Without those relations, I fall back on contact with children, with terrible consequences. I have discussed this with other paedophiles and they also speak of being outside the community while they are offending and not being caught. What the *News of the World* was saying was 'you are not part of the community and we are going to make sure that you stay beyond the pale." Well, for people like me, that's just crazy.

And let's not forget that people like Gerald, not the dangerous predators such as Robert Oliver and Sydney Cooke, make up the vast majority of convicted paedophiles.

There are other issues which it is most doubtful that the *News of the World* considered in its blinkered campaign for a "Sarah's Law" but which, in the real world of public protection, needed to be addressed. For example, on 22 August 2000, the Home Office minister of state, Paul Boateng, received a letter from the assistant chief probation officer of Dorset, alerting him to contingency plans which were being drawn up in the event of vigilante attacks on probation and bail hostels housing paedophiles. There were only two such hostels in the county, and the letter makes clear that, "given the high rate of occupancy of hostels, it is most unlikely that the residents moved out could be accommodated in the south-west". The conclusion was that there should be a national strategy – though there is no sign that one was being developed at the Home Office.

The *News of the World* was also seemingly unaware of, or unconcerned about, the potential impact its campaign would have on compliance of released paedophiles with the Sex Offender Register. Since the requirement to register became law under the 1997 Sex Offenders Act, the national rate of compliance in England and Wales has been encouragingly high. According to the latest Home Office research, it is 94.7 per cent (a figure quoted more recently puts it even higher, at 97 per cent). By contrast, in the United States, the compliance rate with the various state versions of "Megan's Law" is rather lower. For example, the highest level of compliance is almost certainly in Washington state, which has had a law on the statute book since 1992, and there the figure is 84 per cent (NSPCC, 2001).

When the last Conservative government was planning the legislation which was to become the 1997 Sex Offenders Act, it took account of the American experience and ruled out a home-grown version of "Megan's Law". In an interview with the authors, Michael Howard, home secretary until the 1997 general election (now shadow chancellor), explained why: "I was not in favour of a 'Megan's Law'. I took the view that if information on a child sex offender was going to be made public, the temptation for him to evade the law and not register would be that much greater because one factor in his mind would be the fear about that information being publicly available. Frankly, publishing such information would be tantamount to inviting vigilante activity. I thought it best – and I still do – that the police should decide who ought to be given information about a released paedophile."

And naming and shaming? "I am not in favour of telling the whole world about a paedophile's past after they have been released (though neither am I in favour of protecting a paedophile's identity when convicted). If there is a link between naming and shaming and vigilante activity, then it is to be deplored. You cannot allow people to take the law into their own hands. You have to resist that – it is one of the hallmarks of a civilized society to do so." Whatever one's views about Michael Howard as home secretary, he could hardly be accused of being "soft" on public protection.

The local press

The events of July and August 2000 provoked a "feeding frenzy" in the media. For at least six weeks, anything with a connection to paedophiles, however remote, was guaranteed space in the newspapers and on air. And though the *News of the World* undoubtedly heightened the tempo by its naming and shaming campaign, it is only fair to record that there was already intense press coverage, triggered by the abduction of Sarah Payne, before the *News of the World* edition of 23 July. And this is true both at a national and a local level. The following example shows how the response of one regional editor had serious implications for the public protection agencies, notably the police.

During the afternoon of 11 July, a reporter from the *Peterborough Evening Telegraph* rang the press office of Cambridgeshire Police, wanting to know details of a case which had come up several days earlier at Peterborough Crown Court but which had not been reported. The journalist said his interest had been aroused by a call from a resident, who had been "most upset" that one of her neighbours, a 67-year-old man named Billy Baker, had been given a three-year probation order for indecently assaulting four young children. The caller had said she was aggrieved on two counts. First, that the sentence had been far too lenient. Second, that the offender had not been named and shamed in the local press.

At this point, it is important to know that Cambridgeshire Police had, for many years, had a protocol with the regional media in East Anglia to cover the treatment of potentially sensitive issues such as released sex offenders. Initiated by the force's then head of corporate information, Matt Tapp, the agreement had worked successfully since the mid-1990s. "We had a verbal understanding that if a journalist got wind of something which had the potential to cause problems, he or she would ring us first and we would give as much information as we could. It certainly wasn't an attempt to stifle the media but to provide context. For instance, if a reporter had had a call from a bloke at no. 35 saying there was a paedophile living next door, we would point out that, yes, it was true, but it was a minor offence and the conviction was spent in any case. I held meetings with editors, TV and radio station managers, etc., about four times a year to monitor how things were working. And it's fair to say there was never a serious breach of trust on either side." That is, until the Billy Baker affair.

The police supplied the reporter from the *Peterborough Evening Telegraph* with details about Baker's court appearance – along with a "health warning". At the time of the offences, Baker had been living at a sheltered housing complex for the elderly. His victims were the grandchildren of some of his neighbours and, understandably, he had asked to be moved to another address for his own safety after he had been arrested and charged. Under the terms of the media protocol, Matt Tapp's press office gave advice to the reporter. "We said to him: 'go ahead and publish a story by all means if you think it is in the public interest. We have no problem with that, but, in the current climate, disclosing the exact address is almost bound to lead to vigilante trouble.'"

The following day, 12 July, the front page of the *Peterborough Evening Telegraph* was dominated by a banner headline: "The Enemy Within", accompanied by a photograph of Baker "snatched" on the doorstep of his home. The street name appeared on page 2, alongside this comment from the grandmother of one of the victims: "If I get hold of Baker, I will kill him." Within hours of the newspaper appearing, posters were being fixed to lampposts and telegraph poles near Baker's flat, bearing the same photo of him. One said: "This man is a child abuser. He is living at 151 Kesteven Walk. Do not let your child out of your sight until this man is gone!!!" Predictably, a large and threatening crowd began to form outside the flat, and the police, in consultation with housing officials, took the decision to move Baker to a place of safety.

Matt Tapp wrote immediately to the editor of the *Peterborough Evening Telegraph*, Kevin Booth, pointing out his concern at what had happened. "They published Baker's name and photograph. So he had been shamed in the most public way possible. What was the point in publishing his address? It was clearly going to encourage vigilantes and, to my mind, was plainly irresponsible." On 13 July, the editor defended his decision in a leader article. These are excerpts from it. Our comments are in italics.

Eighteen months ago, there wouldn't have been a newspaper editor in this country who would have hesitated for one second before publishing the story. After all, people who are fined for motoring offences or fail to pay their TV licence get their name and address in the local newspaper. Why shouldn't this man?

Even allowing for the dubious proposition that, before the Sydney Cooke affair, every local and regional paper would automatically have published a story about a man convicted of indecent assault, how many would have given it the prominence and inflammatory headline which the PET did? And to ask how this conviction differs in loss of public esteem from a fine for watching a TV without a licence beggars belief.

... there is also the more emotional issue of a local newspaper's responsibility to its readers. If a man is convicted of four charges of indecent assault and we don't report it, what about the risk to children in his locality? What if he offends again and we have covered up his presence? What price our public service then?

> *To suggest that publishing a name and photo (but without an address) is a "cover-up" is absurd. And the sententious comment about providing a "public service", when, as far as we are aware, the Peterborough Evening Telegraph is run as a wholly commercial venture, is merely a figleaf for a course of action which was pretty well indefensible.*

What reinforces our view that the paper was clutching at every available straw to justify itself is its recourse, several days later, to that hoary old cliché the readers poll. The results were trumpeted under the headline "PET backed in name and shame poll", and the story said that 88 per cent of callers in a telephone poll agreed with the decision to run the Billy Baker story. Matt Tapp's take on that is somewhat different: "I gather that only about 90 people actually rang the telephone hotline to express a view. Considering that the circulation of the *PET* is about 24,000, I would hardly call that a ringing endorsement."

There is an interesting parallel here with the *News of the World*'s own use of opinion-poll results to bolster its controversial campaign. On 20 August, the paper proclaimed on its front page the results of a MORI poll. The headline read: "82 per cent of Britain wants Sarah's Law". An analysis three days later in *The Guardian* described this conclusion as follows: "Even in the dismal history of newspaper coverage of specially commissioned opinion polls, this must stand out as one of the most remarkable pieces of selective reporting and amnesia in the cause of self-justification." The reason for its scorn was the paper's failure to mention that, in response to the question: "Was the *NoW* right or wrong to pursue a policy of naming and shaming?", 51 per cent said it was wrong. And, on Sarah's Law, the wording of the question was so loaded as to be quite obviously designed to elicit an overwhelmingly positive response.

Conclusion

The *News of the World* distributed widely a press pack in support of its campaign for new paedophile legislation. On the front page, above a photo of Sarah Payne, are the words: "A Sarah's Law might have saved my life." It is a challenging thought – but characteristically wrong-headed. Of course her murder by Roy Whiting was a wicked act and devastated the lives of her family and all those who knew her. But the failure lay not in keeping the local community in the dark about Whiting's presence but in the fact that, having already served a prison term for abducting a child, he was set free after only two years to strike again. Moreover, set free without having even been on the prison service Sex Offender Treatment Programme to confront his deviancy. It is also astonishing that the judge at Whiting's trial for that earlier crime accepted the defence plea that a rope and a knife found in the boot of his car were not evidence of premeditation. And it is clearly unacceptable that, as the law stood at the time of Whiting's release in 1995, he was subject to probation supervision for only four months.

But in what way would a "Sarah's Law" have made any difference to her tragic fate? If Sara and Michael Payne had known of the existence of Roy Whiting, would they have forbidden their children to play together in a cornfield some distance from where he lived? The depressing fact is that, unless the Roy Whitings of this world are imprisoned for the rest of their natural lives, a child somewhere will always be at risk.

Yes, it is true that the *News of the World* eventually broadened its campaign to include other measures which found their way into strengthened sex offender legislation in the autumn of 2000 – such as the requirement for offenders to register within seventy-two hours of release rather than a fortnight and to do so in person at a police station. But, as Gill Mackenzie points out, these changes were in the pipeline and would have happened anyway. The most, she says, that the *News of the World* can justifiably claim is that it helped accelerate that process. But at what price? "Yes, the *NoW* highlighted a serious issue. But they did it in a violent and unyielding way which did more harm than good. They gave parents false ideas about where the real risk to their children lay. They disrupted the treatment of paedophiles and thus increased the risk to the community. They created a climate of vigilantism and lawlessness and caused pain and suffering to innocent people. Did any of that contribute to the protection of our children? It did not."

9

"Charlie's Angels" and How to Protect our Children

They photocopied Charlie's picture and put a copy on the desks of every schoolchild in Ontario, with a list of his crimes. They put a copy on the desk of our son, Matthew. He said to the teacher, "This man was having supper with us last night", and you can imagine the reaction. Charlie was under 24-hour police surveillance for six weeks, and I later found out that this cost $300,000. How on earth they have come to have this much influence on the criminal justice system is bizarre. These "icons of horror" are just pathetic men. It was really just accidental courage that led me to set up the first Circle, and I jokingly called ourselves "Charlie's Angels".

Pastor Harry Nigh

Without the Circles of Support we couldn't do our job. It's as simple as that – they are there 24/7.

Detective Brian Thomson, Toronto Sexual Abuse Squad

Introduction

In this final chapter, we extend our horizons and look to North America to see what lessons may be learned for the monitoring and supervision of paedophiles in the community. We find positive news in one project, which began in Canada and now has a deserved toehold in the UK. And we discover no empirical evidence that the so-called Megan's Law has contributed anything at all to child protection in the United States, and thus it should not become the model for legislation in the UK. We use this journey beyond our

167

shores to buttress our central argument that risk management of paedophiles begins at home – sometimes, literally – and that it cannot
be achieved by isolating, excluding or, worse, persecuting them.

We begin with a unique project in Toronto called Circles of
Support and Accountability, which survives precariously on a small
grant from the Correctional Service of Canada administered by the
Mennonite Church. For the last eight years, this community-based,
volunteer-run project has been working with released paedophiles
returning from prison to live in the community, by helping the
offender find a place to live, and dealing with the media, the police
and angry community activists. We visited Toronto to watch several
Circles in action, and present here, for the first time, impressions of
the project, as well as evaluations by psychologists and criminologists. These make striking reading, for preliminary research suggests
that, with "high risk" released paedophiles, the Circles have reduced
predicted reoffending by over 60 per cent.

Our guide was the key coordinator of the project, Eileen
Henderson. With her, we visited prisons and churches, attended
AA meetings, sat in on several Circles, ate numerous meals and
drank too many cups of coffee, and talked to scores of volunteers –
everyday Canadian "soccer mums and dads" – as well as psychologists
from the Canadian Correctional Service and police officers from
Toronto's Sexual Abuse Squad. The aim was to discover not only
how, but also why, Circles "worked". What was it that the Canadians
had discovered, and that we in turn could learn, about protecting
our children from the threat of predatory paedophiles? We spoke
at length to Detective Wendy Leaver, who is unique in that she not
only works on the Sexual Abuse Squad but is also a member of
a Circle, and to Robin Wilson, director of the Sexual Behaviour
Program for the Correctional Service of Canada, who has written
about Circles. Finally, we met several "core members" of the Circles
– the paedophiles themselves – to find out why they felt this idea
had succeeded when other interventions had failed.

A short history of Circles of Support and Accountability (Circles)

Circles began in 1994 when Pastor Harry Nigh and some of his
church members chose to become involved with Charlie, and to

help him to resettle in a community – Hamilton, Ontario – that was both scared and angry. Harry describes his decision to do so as "accidental courage", but he had at least been used to working with offenders in prisons, and knew of Charlie from his ministry inside. In short, he knew Charlie before he was released, and remembers receiving a phone call from the psychologist at the prison asking if he could help Charlie when he reached "warrant expiry" – in effect, the final date that he could be legally incarcerated. "I remember that I just wanted to help him ease the transition from custody, and perhaps help him find accommodation." Harry also recalls that Charlie was "illiterate, had never worked – in fact he's unemployable, and has an IQ of about 70." Even so, as Harry explains, the decision to form a Circle around Charlie was as much about "not knowing of a way to get out of it" as anything else, and very soon he and his wife Shirley found themselves "in the midst of something that we had no real idea about". However, he remembered a method of working with people who were mentally ill, which involved a circle of six people gathering around that person, so that every day one circle member would make contact and support them. On the seventh day everyone would get together and share a meal.

This was the model that was to be adopted by the Circles in their work with paedophiles, even though in the beginning Harry had no idea that it would be replicated elsewhere. In effect, each day a member of the Circle will visit the "core member", both to support him and to hold him accountable for his attitudes and actions within the community. The goal of the Circles – as they have developed – is not therapeutic, but rather to provide support and accountability. As such the Circles represent a shift away from the cognitive behavioural approach of the SOTP and a traditional reliance on professional expertise. For while police officers and other professionals can join, in the main Circles draw on the latent skills of community volunteers – who initially, but not exclusively, came from the faith community. In all of this there are clear elements of what is known as "restorative justice", which seeks to acknowledge the harm that has been done to the victims of crime, but at the same time attempts to work with the offender and the community so as to prevent further victimization.

The Circle thus works on a daily basis in informal gatherings in coffee shops and diners, on the telephone, and at other key events or venues in the core member's life. As Robin Wilson explained, training is provided to those who volunteer to work within the

Table 9.1   The 5 'C's of Circles

Circles	Not one-to-one relationships
Consensus	Not custodial or authoritarian
Covenant	Responsibility and accountability
Celebration	Of important milestones
Community	Based and focused; not institutional

Circle, and there is a shared understanding of what it is that is expected of a volunteer that is expressed as the "5 'C's of Circles" (see table 9.1). The Circle can interact with professionals who are involved with the core member in order to support that core member better and to hold him accountable. The Circle can advocate on behalf of the core member, but at the same time it will confront him about attitudes and behaviour – especially behaviour that is seen to be offence-specific. Similarly, a Circle will mediate in situations of conflict between the community and the core member, or, as Harry Nigh explained, "to walk with the core member through crises and problems". There is also a focus on celebration; of marking each positive step that the core member is able to take within the community. Again this echoes themes within "restorative justice", which would suggest that, for there to be any successful reintegration of offenders into the community, there must be active participation of the community with the offender. The intended result is to reduce reoffending through deterrence and prevention, rather than relying on punishment.

Circles in action

What follows is an account of a Circle in action, observed in the summer of 2001 and written up by one of the authors from extensive contemporaneous notes. The present tense has been used deliberately to convey the immediacy of the experience.

Eileen Henderson looks like the typical Canadian "soccer mum" so loved by advertising agencies. She is married to Randy, and they live in a prosperous, middle-class suburb of Toronto with their two children – Matt, who at seventeen listens to British indie-rock and has just got his driving licence, and Alannah, who, like most Canadian girls of fourteen, has braces on her teeth, a dog and a rather worrying fondness for S Club 7, and plays soccer for her school.

Tonight Eileen has left Randy and the kids at home and invited me instead to a meeting in the very pleasant middle-class house of one of her colleagues, surrounded by four of their friends who are discussing Ezra Pound, abstract art and contemporary American cinema – over ice cream, home-made pie and "real" coffee. Oh yes, and there is another guest – in fact he's the centre of attention.

For, despite this seemingly relentlessly ordinary background, Eileen is anything but typical. Few "soccer mums" devote their lives to working with "warrant expired" paedophiles (i.e., paedophiles who have reached the end of their prison sentence and are to be released back into the community) through a concept inspired by a mental health development. Eileen is project manager of this initiative, which emerged from a series of chance circumstances and is now formalized and sponsored by the Mennonite Church. Put simply, it involves forming a "circle" of six everyday people around the released paedophile, who becomes known as the "core member". The members of the circle not only hold him accountable for his behaviour in the community, but also act as advocates to secure counselling and welfare for him, ensuring that he has accommodation, is looking for work, and has been eating regularly. No worries tonight – he's just had second helpings of ice cream.

Just think about this for a moment and get a sense of what these circles are all about and which we're witnessing for the first time. Can you imagine forming a close daily relationship with these "icons of horror", as they have been described to us, risking your nice, ordinary and comfortable life for a group of offenders who have caused untold damage to the most vulnerable members of the community? Can you imagine taking them for lunch, driving them around town to find accommodation, attending their AA meetings with them, and generally being available for them on a twenty-four hour a day basis? Why on earth would anyone want to do that?

The following day, as we leave Pound, Joseph Albers and the merits of the new *Planet of the Apes* behind us, we drive out of Toronto to Warkworth Institution – some three hours north of the city, to interview two about-to-be-released paedophiles around whom a Circle will be formed. Eileen explains to me why she first became involved in Circles and why she does what she does.

171

I do it because I firmly believe that I've been blessed in my life and all of us have a responsibility to put back into the community – to give to the community. Sure, I have a faith, and that faith makes me see people – all people – as worthwhile.

"Even paedophiles?" I ask. "Even people like Pal, the first 'core member' in Toronto, who abused over 30 kids by getting them to pretend that they were in a Nazi death camp where he was the doctor, and would have them moan and scream so as to help him achieve an erection?" Eileen fixes me with a warm smile, as if to say that she's been asked this question before, but she answers nonetheless.

We do not have the power to act as judge and jury as to who is valuable and who is not – even paedophiles. And if the Circles can stop others from being abused, while at the same time giving the offender a sense that people do care, that they are not isolated or excluded, that they are not programmed to offend, but have choices, then that seems to me to be not just the right thing to do, but a good thing to do.

This might seem too trite for our British sensibilities, until you begin to realize that this isn't just simple Christian theorizing but the basis for a programme of action that has won the support of the Canadian Correctional Service and Toronto's Sexual Abuse Squad. One officer on the squad, Detective Constable Brian Thomson, for example – as traditional a "cop" as you could ever hope to find on either side of the Atlantic – puts it quite simply when he tells me that "without the Circles we could not do our job." He goes on to explain that "they are there 24/7", something which he feels that he can't be, as "I have to give a sense of authority."

However, Wendy Leaver takes a different view and, despite being a police officer herself, and a colleague of Thomson's, is a member of Pal's Circle. When asked to join, she admits that her first reaction was, "What? I put these guys in jail". And that at the first meeting of the Circle she kept thinking that "they don't know what paedophiles are about – there is no cure for paedophilia." But she stuck with it – in fact she now pays personally for his daily "meals on wheels" – and can now reflect on Pal's last seven years in the community.

Without us, he'd have offended again. I want to keep my community safe. OK, I'm a police officer and this is hardly a prized volunteer job – no one is going to pat you on the back – but we need to support sex offenders or paedophiles or we leave the door open to recidivism.

It's clear that views like these have not necessarily gone down well with some of her colleagues, who see them as too "touchy-feely", and Wendy remembers that, in the early days of Pal's Circle, they would hang banners on the wall of her office saying "Who are you going to lunch with today?" But increasingly she can point to evidence to support her Circle's work. The first empirical evaluation of the first thirty circles formed in Canada is just being produced, and the report's author – Dr Robin Wilson of the Correctional Service of Canada – tells me that recidivism in what is undoubtedly a "high risk group" currently stands at less than 40 per cent of the predicted reoffending rate – a phenomenally positive result for this type of offender.

So what is it about the Circles that works? On our seemingly never-ending journey to Warkworth Institution, Eileen ponders the question. "I think it's about people forming a community, and not excluding anyone. Looking at everyone as people." This idea of "community" was at the heart of what every circle member would describe to me when I asked them this question, and Eileen articulates it.

> The majority of these men have been abused as well as abusers, and they are usually isolated and alone. The idea of community is therefore very different for them. Sometimes I get the feeling that they are like children, and that we are their family and that they'd disappoint us if they reoffended. That's it, I think – they don't want to disappoint us.

This idea of "belonging to a family" and being accepted takes on greater significance when Wendy Leaver reminds me that Pal had to be released from prison in the boot of a Circle member's car – so great was the media coverage.

> The paedophile comes into the community with huge media hype, which merely reinforces his crimes. If you bring them into a Circle what you do is calm the community down – although there is still very little understanding – and they learn that they have support. That's important because in the jail this type of offender has been the lowest of the low; he hears from the media what life is going to be like on the outside; they have no family and he's a person we've learned to hate. So if he comes

out with no support, the recidivism rates are fulfilled. The Circle presents them with a built-in, if reluctant, family.

Pal himself says much the same when I interview him over a meal before he attends an AA meeting with his Circle. Face to face, it is difficult to imagine how this weedy, needy and essentially powerless man could have exercised such a hold over the collective imagination and the workings of the Canadian criminal justice system. Nonetheless he remembers that he was "public enemy number one" and says that it is "hard to put into words what my Circle did, but they were there for everything – the good times and the crises. I'm in phone contact almost every day with Eileen, and she is an ear to listen to my whining and complaining. They found me accommodation, and have basically supported me like a family."

At last we are reaching Warkworth, and Eileen is preparing to go into the prison when her phone rings. It's her daughter Alannah – she's just scored a goal in the school soccer competition.

Eileen goes through the formalities of entering the jail and I'm left wondering if Britain, despite two or three pilot projects, is ready to embrace the idea of Circles of Support, or whether we are still too concerned that there is nothing that can be done with these "icons of horror" other than keeping them locked up forever, even after they are "warrant expired", like those who live in the specially created hostel within the grounds of HMP Nottingham. If that's so, more fool us, for, as Eileen says, "Circles are as much about us – the community – as they are about offenders, and if they work, then surely they are the right thing to do, not just for the paedophile, but also for us?"

Taking it all one stage further

There are at least three inter-related but distinct reasons that Circle members offer when asked why they volunteer to give up their spare time to work with the core members. These are faith, human rights, and "making the community safer". Of course, these are not mutually exclusive categories, and some volunteers mentioned aspects of all three in answering questions about their motivations. Rick, for example, explained that he volunteered because "all my idealism and beliefs aside, it just seems right. The faith aspect is important to me, and my Christian beliefs make what I'm doing more meaningful, but this is also about making things safer." Several others also found their way into the Circles via a church network, and, crucially, several prominent clerics participate in the programme. We have already described Pastor Harry Nigh's involvement, and the support given to the Circles by the Mennonite Central Committee, but others such as the Reverend Hugh Kirkegaard also took up the cause. As he explained, "I did it originally because it was part of my work as a community chaplain", although other issues were to surface for him which reinforced his commitment to the Circles. However, perhaps Wendy Leaver put this faith issue at its most basic when she observed: "who else would deal with these people if it wasn't for the Christian community?"

Although Hugh Kirkegaard initially became involved through his work as a chaplain, he quickly came to see that "there are human rights issues too – both for the offenders and for the community." In relation to the former, he thought that the police in Toronto were initially "treating these people not as citizens, but as perpetual offenders. They'd done their time, but they weren't being allowed to function in the community in any real way." This is an important observation, and one that we develop further when we consider why Circles work. Similarly, Malcolm Savage – another Circle member – describes his volunteering as a "social responsibility", and Eileen Henderson thought that "this is how people should respond generally to other people – to see people as people and not as 'things'." She went further, and described her Circle as "a small bonfire, throwing some light into the darkness. It stops people becoming victims and gives the offender an insight that people do care, and they can make choices not to offend."

This idea of "social responsibility" also involves holding the offender accountable for his actions, and so, for example, Hugh Kirkegaard remembers some difficult times with Pal.

> We really challenged him about his drinking – he'd go on benders, and then he'd look for kids. We didn't particularly like him, but we had to support him if we were going to make him accountable, and in making him account for his behaviour we were also making the community safer.

Pal's drinking was thus of particular concern, and at first he was not motivated to change. Hugh Kirkegaard describes, for example, one particular crisis.

After a few months his room-mate called me and told me that Pal was drinking again – in fact he'd passed out on the floor of the apartment. I lived not far away, and I called a couple of other Circle members and we went over there. We suspected that he'd been drinking for months. We are in a relationship dynamic with him, not a custodial one, and we just sat down and were really at the limit of our resources. He needed a wake-up call and that's why we called Wendy Leaver, and we put him in jail for the weekend.

This "wake-up call" is perhaps unusual, given how relatively extreme it is, and reflects the fact that, in those early days, Circle members were just developing their awareness of how to work with the core members. Nonetheless, it worked, and as part of the research for the book we attended an AA meeting with Pal, and a celebratory meal beforehand.

For other core members, being held accountable involves finding appropriate work, or accommodation, or perhaps simply ensuring that they stay within budget over a particular time period. This accountability is sometimes linked with their offending history – as it was with Pal's drinking – but can often be simply about helping them to function better as responsible community members. In this respect, the Circle members become role models in how to deal with people, both within and outside of the Circle, and how to manage the inevitable problems that will occur from time to time.

Surprisingly, the most common reason given for volunteering was a desire to "make the community safer" by putting something positive back into it. This is surprising, because the volunteers are not professional therapists and, with the exception of one or two, have had no experience either of the criminal justice system in general, or with sex offenders or paedophiles in particular. As Hugh Kirkegaard explains, there was a great deal of naivety about all of this – especially in the beginning: "I just didn't know what I was getting into . . . I was in way over my head, but we formed a Circle anyway." So what is it that is being given that might make the community safer? Hugh Kirkegaard again: "What we are offering these offenders is a relationship rather than custody. They have never functioned successfully in the community before and they need our help to do so." He goes on to explain that "the bottom line is that these people are not monsters sent from another planet. They came out of our communities and we have to find ways of working with them in the community while at the same time keeping that community safe."

So, does it work? Dr Robin Wilson, director of the Sexual Behaviour Program for the Correctional Service of Canada, is the most authoritative source on the success or otherwise of the Circles. He made his most recent research available to us (it has still to be published, but is written in conjunction with Michelle Prinzo). It looked at thirty high-risk sexual offenders released at sentence completion (a group which includes Charlie and Pal), all of whom had become part of a Circle. The average length of membership of a Circle was thirty-six months, but their participation ranged from sixteen to seventy-nine months. Wilson used two actuarial measures – the Rapid Risk Assessment of Sex Offender Recidivism and the Structured Anchored Clinical Judgement – to predict violent recidivism among this group. Mean time risk was thirty-six months, but with a range from sixteen months to just over six and half years, and Wilson calculated that there would have been approximately seven instances of sexual recidivism within this group at the date of his research. However, only three of this group had reoffended: one had made indecent phone calls, another had committed an offence against a child, and the third had sexually assaulted a female adult. In each case the offence category was less serious than the crime for which the offender had previously served a custodial sentence. Thus Wilson concludes that Circle members are reoffending at a rate of less than 40 per cent of that which is predicted by the actuarial scales.

With this type of offender this is a significant and surprising finding – especially as the model adopted within the Circle is not custodial or therapeutic, but simply about forging relationships. In short, Circles, unlike the SOTP, have nothing overtly to do with cognitive skills, behavioural modification, and deviancy control and are not run by professionals. Indeed, in one sense they are "anti-professional", and rely instead on the ability of the volunteer Circle members to effect change and control, over telephone calls, meals, and trips to the cinema. But why should this work – especially when other interventions have failed in the past? We asked Circle members why they thought that the Circles succeeded, and then triangulated their observations by discussing what they had said with the core members themselves. The Circle members offered one consistent and overwhelming reason – a reason which goes to the heart of the questions which we have posed throughout this book, and which has implications for the development of policy in our own country.

Consider the following two observations – the first by Hugh Kirkegaard, and the second by Eileen Henderson:

He hasn't reoffended because he's discovered for the first time that he's wanted. We've become the first real family that he's ever had. He's found a group of people who were prepared to walk with him, care for him, and stand by him when he screws up. Of course he's "high risk". But the irony of that definition is that when you put pressure on that type of person their risk levels increase dramatically – they return to familiar patterns of offending when they are under stress.

It's all about people forming and creating community, and not excluding anyone. It's about looking at people as people. The majority of the men are usually isolated and therefore community is very different for them. You know I get the feeling that they'd disappoint us if they reoffended, and they don't want to disappoint us because we are family.

These observations that the Circles become "family" and represent "inclusiveness", and through this a way of preventing the paedophile from reoffending, are given added weight by Wendy Leaver from her understanding as a Circle member, and also as a police officer. She explains:

The Circle presents him with a built-in and perhaps reluctant family. Six individuals who accept him as he is . . . we all start talking to each other and a family develops, and we start sharing experiences. Eventually you let him forget his offences, and let him speak about himself. We let him start talking about his basic needs . . . the core member is initially taken aback, but then he begins to realize that no one wants anything to do with him, and when there's awful media coverage, all of a sudden you'll get a phone call from the core member and the Circle will meet, and he feels safe. The key thing is the acceptance of that individual as a member of society – a contributing member – not as a paedophile, who has only and will only ever have that label. If you don't let them forget that, then that's all they will ever be – a paedophile.

The views of the Circle members are echoed by the core members, and Pal, for example, admits: "I'd have messed up several times if it hadn't been for my Circle." When asked to explain what it is that the Circle provides, he pauses, and tries to find the right words:

They are there for everything – the good times and the crises. It is a friendship thing, and I suppose I'm in daily contact with Eileen and

178

one or two others. My Circle is my life-saver – that's the only way
that I can describe it. Now, I like the fact that I've come through all
of this without reoffending, and with my mental health good, and of
course I now have friends. I'm not proud of what I did, but now I just
want to move on and be given the chance to be helpful to others.

We give the last word on the Circles to Wendy Leaver – appropriately, because, in framing her thoughts, she goes to the heart of
the matter.

You know we can't afford to lock them all up, and even if we could
afford it financially, is that the sort of society we would want to
become? Look at what you are doing in England! They are having to
go back to prison for safety! Do you really want to live in a society
based on the law of the vigilante? If we do that with paedophiles,
why not drug dealers and burglars?

Megan's Law

It should be clear by now that those ideas for managing the risk
posed by paedophiles in the community which we support are those
that can be shown to work and with which society feels comfortable. Castrating paedophiles would fail both tests, and, while prison
undoubtedly protects society for a limited period, there are not
enough jails, or sufficient resources to build them, to house the
huge number of people who sexually abuse children, even if it was
possible to catch and convict them all. So it is the pragmatist in
us which sees such exciting potential in the Circles of Support.
The fact that it also seems right for the community to take responsibility for protecting itself in such a positive way is an ethical
bonus.

But we recognize that, for many, perhaps the majority, both in
the UK and North America, such an inclusive approach is untenable
and appears to be some kind of a betrayal of abused children. For
them, involving the community has a different meaning: as a retri-
butive need, and as a natural reflex based upon the belief that little
can be done to change the way paedophiles behave, and that therefore society must "empower" itself with knowledge – knowing where
the perpetrators live and what they look like. This is the exclusive
approach which sees the paedophile as an alien other who has to be

rendered harmless by fear of exposure or worse. In the UK, it has been called Sarah's Law, after the murdered Sarah Payne. However, that soubriquet is a borrowing from the United States, where every state has a so-called Megan's Law in recognition of Megan Kanka, who was abducted and murdered in New Jersey in 1994 by a released paedophile who, unbeknown to Megan's family, lived across the street. Put simply, since 1996, all fifty states and the District of Columbia have had a law on their statute books which authorizes the release of information to the public about those on the Sex Offender Register (not just paedophiles). It is not a discretionary requirement but a mandatory one.

In February 2001, the *News of the World* organized a meeting in the Grand Committee Room of the House of Commons to press its political campaign for Sarah's Law. The meeting was addressed by Sarah Payne's mother, Sara, as well as the editor of the *News of the World*, Rebekah Wade, who sought to make a distinction between her proposed legislation and Megan's Law. She said: "We want *controlled* public access to information about convicted sex offenders rather than Megan's Law, which is community notification and carries a big price tag." She was not asked what she meant by that last phrase. Whether it was an allusion to a financial cost or the social cost of vigilante behaviour, rehousing of paedophiles who had been "outed", and so on. One of the chief speakers at the meeting was the New Jersey senator Peter Inverso, who – according to the press handout prepared by the *News of the World* – "would inform politicians about the success of Megan's Law", which he had helped to draft and push through the state legislature only eighty-nine days after Megan Kanka's death. Senator Inverso duly told his audience of about fifteen MPs that, "across the United States, there has been a decline in the number of sex crimes against children since the implementation of Megan's Law, with New Jersey leading the way."

Senator Inverso's assurance and the forceful advocacy of the *News of the World* of a version of Megan's Law, even if not exactly the same in every detail, is designed to give the impression that the UK would be importing legislation which had been shown to be effective in improving the protection of children over almost a decade in the United States. In fact, nothing could be further from the truth, as the NSPCC has shown in a timely evaluation of community notification as it has applied in the USA since the early 1990s. The findings make salutary reading.

Given that the enactment of Megan's Law – and its predecessor legislation in a number of states where there had been high-profile child murders since 1990 – was a response to the crimes of predatory paedophiles, it is reasonable to ask whether it has helped reduce the number of such attacks. But no states appear to keep figures for "stranger" assaults, including New Jersey, so it is impossible to draw any conclusions about this key issue. Such evidence as there is certainly does not make out an overwhelming case for the "success" of community notification. Take Washington state, for example, which, as we have pointed out elsewhere, has one of the highest rates of compliance with the requirement to register as a convicted sex offender. The NSPCC study quotes a 1995 state study, done before Washington's version of the federal Megan's Law was enacted, which shows that 22 per cent of sex offenders who had been arrested had reoffended. After the law went into effect, it was 19 per cent. The difference is not regarded as statistically significant. (And it should be borne in mind that any fall in the statistics for sex crime has to be seen in the context of an overall downward trend in violent crime in many parts of the United States. Therefore to isolate the impact of one specific piece of legislation is a dubious proposition.)

There is little or no data on how community notification "empowers" parents, as its advocates on both sides of the Atlantic argue, or on the ways in which parents use this information to protect children. No research appears to have been done on whether sex offenders have been driven "underground". And there is little knowledge about whether and how adults and children change their behaviour as a result of community notification. It is also right to point out that there is no solid evidence that misuse of information as a result of mandatory community notification has led to increased harassment, vigilantism or blackmail. As the NSPCC report shows, on every index of assessment about a policy which has preoccupied opinion-formers in the UK for the best part of two years, almost nothing has been added to the state of our knowledge during a decade of use in the United States. Its conclusion that "there is clearly a need for further research" is a masterly understatement.

In contrast to what we do not know about the impact of Megan's Law, we do know what happened in the UK when the *News of the World* embarked on its naming and shaming campaign. We know that it led to the most unsavoury brand of do-it-yourself "justice" and that it heightened the risk to the community by frightening some paedophiles into fleeing from their homes and abandoning their supervisory arrangements by police or probation.

We do not find it surprising that the United States has been so comprehensively seduced by community notification, despite the absence of any evidence to show that it works. A nation which imprisons more than two million of its citizens and which has invested so heavily in a "penal-industrial" complex is self-evidently one which reaches unthinkingly for criminal justice policies that can be sold to the voters as comforting soundbites rather than subjected to careful analysis. But the sooner it is acknowledged that this has little to do with child protection, the better it will be for all of us.

Concluding thoughts

This book was conceived out of a desire to inform, not to preach. There are enough people bellowing from soap boxes – or their more comfortable equivalent, the newspaper column – about how to protect society and cut crime without adding to the clamour. What has been lacking is a measured attempt to distinguish between those strategies which can make us safer and more self-aware and those which simply make us feel better. Where we pillory arguments, it is because those propounding them have deliberately distorted the facts or tried to manipulate opinion by exploiting fear and prejudice. Since child sex abuse itself is all about exploitation and manipulation, it is an irony seemingly lost on these people.

Many of the questions we have asked in this book have been relatively easy to pose – from what happens to a paedophile in prison, to why they do what they do, and to whether they can be treated. The answers could often be provided by simple description, and by first-hand account, not only from the victims of sexual abuse, but also from those who work with paedophiles in prisons and in the community. It is far more difficult to explain our collective collusion with the idea of "stranger danger", when we are all too aware that most children will be abused by someone they know. Or why we have become so concerned with paedophiles at a time when we have sexualized children, especially girls, in our contemporary culture. Given that, overwhelmingly, paedophiles are male, one answer may be found in the crisis of male sexuality which some (predominantly female) observers identify as an increasingly significant social phenomenon. If this had been a book about sociological theory we would have explored this territory at some length, but it isn't, and we make no apologies for concentrating on those practical policies which can make a difference to child protection.

This is why we would rather put our faith in the MAPPPs, Circles of Support and Stop it Now than the vapid sloganizing of the *News of the World* and its acolytes. Unlike some critics of the media, we have not wasted time stating the obvious: that many editions of the tabloids which fulminate against paedophiles and call for draconian punishments also devote a healthy amount of space to a range of other salacious sexual exploits – from fornicating footballers to randy royals. Unfortunately, most of us are guilty of hypocrisy or inconsistency, and this, in itself, does not invalidate a point of view if it is soundly based. Nor have we aimed at easy targets by deriding the protesters of Paulsgrove without giving them time and space to articulate grievances which are deeply held. In this, we believe we have fulfilled our mandate to be fair and explanatory rather than to engage in a self-indulgent polemic.

However, we recognize that this may not shield us from those critics who will see this book as just another parading of liberal *Angst*. "Understand, but never condemn", we can already hear them saying: the discredited mantra of the 1960s and 1970s rehashed for a new century. In fact, the opposite is the case. As we explained in Chapter 4, in the field of criminology, the 1970s, in particular, was the period of "nothing works" – a despairing belief that the pattern of crime was set by certain economic and sociological trends which would defy policy shifts by government, and that it frankly didn't matter what new initiative came out of Whitehall. (Hence the view that community-based punishment was no less likely to succeed in cutting recidivism rates than prison, because crime rates seemed to go up whichever penalty was applied.)

But "nothing works" has itself been discredited, and we subscribe to the prevailing mood in the prisons and probation world, which is expressed as "what works" – in other words, invest your time and resources in those policies which can be demonstrated to make a difference. This is precisely the philosophy which underpins our advocacy of Circles and Stop it Now in the community and aspects of the SOTP in prison. And our dismissal of naming and shaming and community notification. It also means directing our collective energies at the heart of the problem rather than at the periphery. In other words, acknowledging that our children are, statistically, at no greater risk in the year 2002 than they were in 1972 of being abducted and killed by a stranger, but that they remain unacceptably vulnerable to sexual abuse and exploitation by people whom they should be able to trust without question. If we can help correct this corrosive imbalance in society's thinking, we will have achieved our objective.

Bibliography

A.W. Baker and S.P. Duncan (1985): Child sexual abuse: a study of prevalence in Great Britain, *Child Abuse and Neglect*, 9, 457–67.

P. Bebbington (1979): Sexual disorders. In P. Hill, R. Murray and A. Thorley, *Essentials of Postgraduate Psychiatry*. London: Academic Press, 247–76.

A. Beech, D. Fisher, R. Beckett and A. Scott-Fordham (1998): *An Evaluation of the Prison Sex Offender Treatment Programme*. Home Office Research, Development and Statistics Directorate, no. 79.

R. Blackburn (1980): Still not working? A look at some recent outcomes in offender rehabilitation. Paper presented to the Scottish Branch of the British Psychological Society, Conference on Deviance, University of Stirling.

S. Bryans and R. Jones (2001): *Prison and the Prisoner: An Introduction to the Work of HM Prison Service*. London: Stationery Office.

Chartered Institute of Housing (1998): "Rehousing Sex Offenders – A Summary of the Legal and Operational Issues", February, Coventry.

S. Cohen (1972): *Folk Devils and Moral Panics*. London: MacGibbon & Kee.

S. Cohen (1985): *Visions of Social Control*. Cambridge: Polity.

E. Cullen (1995): Grendon: a therapeutic prison that works. *Therapeutic Communities*, 15, 301–11.

M. Foucault (1977): *Discipline and Punish: The Birth of the Modern Prison*. London: Allen Lane.

M. Foucault (1998): *The Will to Knowledge: The History of Sexuality*. Harmondsworth: Penguin.

P. Gendreau and R. Ross (1980): Effective correctional treatment: bibliotherapy for cynics. In R. Ross and P. Gendreau (eds), *Effective Correctional Treatment*. Toronto: Butterworths.

M. Glasser (1989): The psychodynamic approach to understanding and working with the paedophile. In M. Farrell (ed.), *Understanding the Paedophile*. London: ISTD.

Bibliography

D. Grubin (1998): *Sex Offenders Against Children: Understanding the Risk.* Police Research Series, Paper 99, London: Home Office.

E. Guy (1992): Management summary. In *Treatment Programmes for Sex Offenders in Custody: A Strategy.* London: HM Prison Service.

J. Hobson and J. Shine (1998): Measurement of psychopathy in a UK prison population referred for long term psychotherapy. *British Journal of Criminology,* 38, 301–11.

Home Office (1991): *Treatment Programmes for Sex Offenders in Custody: A Strategy.* London: Home Office.

Home Office (1996): *Sentencing and Supervision of Sex Offenders: A Consultation Document.* London: Home Office. cm 3304.

Home Office (1998a): *Exercising Constant Vigilance: The Role of the Probation Service in Protecting the Public from Sex Offenders.* London: Home Office.

Home Office (1998b): *Delivering an Enhanced Level of Community Supervision: Report of a Thematic Inspection on the Work of Approved Probation and Bail Hostels.* London: Home Office.

Home Office (1998c): *The Crime and Disorder Act – Sex Offender Orders: Guidance.* London: Home Office.

Home Office (1999): *The Work of the Probation Services with Sex Offenders.* London: Home Office.

Home Office (2000): *Setting the Boundaries: Reforming the Law on Sex Offences.* London: Home Office.

J. McGuire (2000): *Cognitive-Behavioural Approaches: An Introduction to Theory and Research.* London: Home Office.

J. McGuire and P. Priestley (1985): *Offending Behaviour: Skills and Strategies for Going Straight.* London: Batsford.

P. Marshall (1997): *The Prevalence of Convictions for Sexual Offending,* Research Findings no. 55, Research and Statistics Directorate. London: Home Office.

R. Martinson (1974): What works? Questions and answers about prison reform, *Public Interest,* 35, 22–54.

T. Mathiesen (2001): *Prison on Trial.* Winchester: Waterside Press.

NACRO (1998): *Sex Offenders: Reducing the Risk.* London: NACRO.

NSPCC (2001): "Megan's Law: Does it Protect Children?" July 2001.

G. Pearson (1983): *Hooligan: A History of Respectable Fears.* London: Macmillan.

S. Petrow (1994): *Policing Morals: The Metropolitan Police and the Home Office, 1870–1914.* Oxford: Clarendon Press.

Prison Reform Trust (1990): *Sex Offenders in Prison.* London: PRT.

Prison Reform Trust (1992): *Beyond Containment: The Penal Response to Sex Offending.* London: PRT.

Prison Service (1996): *Sex Offender Treatment Programme: Core Programe Manual.* London: HM Prison Service.

J. Shine and M. Newton (2000): Damaged, disturbed and dangerous: a profile of receptions to Grendon therapeutic prison, 1995–2000. In J. Shine (ed.), *A Compilation of Grendon Research*. PES: Leyhill.

J. Silverman (2000): War crimes inquiries. *History Today*, 50(2), 26–8.

K. Soothill, B. Francis and E. Ackerley (1998): Paedophilia and paedophiles. *New Law Journal*, 882–3.

K. Soothill and C. Walby (1991): *Sex Crimes in the News*. London: Routledge.

T. Thomas (2000): *Sex Crime: Sex Offending and Society*. Cullomptom: Willan Publishing.

R. Webster (1998): *The Great Children's Home Panic*. Oxford: Orwell Press.

D. West (1987): *Sexual Crimes and Confrontations: A Study of Victims and Offenders*. Aldershot: Gower.

L. Wilkins (1964): *Social Deviance*. London: Tavistock.

D. Wilson (1990): HMP Grendon: a maverick prison, *Prison Service Journal*, 87, 18–25.

D. Wilson (1999): Delusions of innocence. In E. Cullen and T. Newell (eds), *Murderers and Life Imprisonment*. Winchester: Waterside Press, 55–72.

D. Wilson and J. Ashton (1998): *What Everyone in Britain Should Know About Crime and Punishment*. Oxford: Oxford University Press.

R. Wyre (1996): The mind of the paedophile. In P. Bibby (ed.), *Organised Abuse: The Current Debate*. Basingstoke: Arena.

Index

188